GIN⁵ OF THE NORTH WEST

THE SPIRIT OF THE LAKES, FELLS, CITIES & COAST

FIONA LAING

GREAT NORTHERN

Fiona Laing is an author and journalist. She has been writing about food and drink for more than a decade and in 2018 started a journey around British gin. First came The GIN CLAN, then YORKSHIRE'S GINS – each providing comprehensive guides to their region's gin. Her interest in drinks started when she worked with the first Indian single malt whisky to launch in Europe. Other spirits and wine were never far behind as she travelled the world, listening to the stories of the makers. Food editor, hotel judge, travel writer, Fiona has explored food and drink whenever her career as a newspaper journalist and PR consultant allowed.

Great Northern Books Limited
PO Box 1380, Bradford, BD5 5FB
www.greatnorthernbooks.co.uk

ISBN: 978-1-914227-29-5

Design and layout: David Burrill

CIP Data
A catalogue for this book is available from the British Library

CONTENTS

THE NORTH WEST OF ENGLAND

The contrasts across the North West of England couldn't be greater. The rural villages and fertile lands of Cheshire in the south and the dramatic fells and lakes of Cumbria in the north bookend the industrial metropolitan heartlands of Liverpool, Manchester and Lancashire. All of this is bordered by the Pennines in the east and the Irish sea to the west.

It is an area rich in inspiration for ginmakers and in the last decade they have capitalised on its bounty in style. They make good use of its natural harvest, dramatic history and industrial resources while calling on the skills and ingenuity of people from all walks of life.

Although the North West is an official region of the UK, it is rather an artificial construct, with few of the cultural or historical links that bind the people in a county such as Yorkshire or Cornwall. Cumbria and the Lake District are so unlike the urban areas of Liverpool and Manchester that talking about them in the same breath is uncomfortable. But what the North West does offer is a wealth of gins, inspired by a range of influences as colourful and exciting as you would expect from a region which is home to more than 7 million people living in both work-hard-play-hard cities and glorious countryside.

There is a strong tradition of distilling in the North West with one of England's first modern gins made at Warrington in the 18th century, Liverpool home to large 19th-century whisky distilleries and Lancashire reputedly a hotbed of illicit whisky making.

The Cheshire market town of Warrington was an important crossing point on the River Mersey and providing hospitality for travellers would have been key to its economy. In 1761, Thomas Dakin bought a small parcel of land on Bridge Street and built a distillery. He pioneered the London Dry method for making gin and when the Greenall family took over his distillery and brewery, the Greenall name was applied to his gin recipe. This makes Greenall's Gin – now part of G&J Distillers' portfolio – the oldest gin in the UK. Today more than 60 million bottles of gin are made a year by G&J Distillers in Warrington.

In the 2010s, as the craft distilling revolution spread across the UK, the first modern distilleries opened in the North West, with five distillers selling their first gins in 2013 or 2014. The growth continued, peaking in 2019, when 15 distilleries opened in the region. Only three set up the next year and four in 2021.

The impact of Covid-19 in 2020 cannot be underestimated. Makers all rely on people socialising – enjoying a gin and tonic with friends and family. Many sell directly to the public at markets, tastings and festivals. They rely on local bars and restaurants stocking their gins. And then there are others who have built a visitor attraction around their distillery. All of this was wiped away in March 2020 as the world shut down.

What is admirable is how ginmakers adapted. Many started making sanitiser, and credit must go to HMRC which allowed distillers to use their alcohol stocks without tying them up in red tape. Ginmakers turned the internet into their best friend with online shops, virtual tastings and cocktail classes developing new ways of doing business. Gins were created to support the hospitality industry and key workers.

What is also interesting is how many people used the lockdown to follow their dreams and there were several gins created and distilleries built in the lean months of 2020. The Wine and Spirit Trade Association reported that gin sales in the UK dropped from £2.7 billion in 2019 to £1.9bn in 2020, but climbed to £2.1bn in 2021. The number of distilleries in England rose by 83 to 311 in 2020 and data from HMRC for 2021 showed that the total climbed again to more than 400.

My research uncovered about 60 distilleries in the region. This is not the number of entries in the distillers' section of this book as some of those businesses are not in operation and a couple have failed to respond to inquiries. So we are left with 55 distilleries in the North West. The gins from brands which do not have their own distillery were particularly hard to tie down, with some saying things were too uncertain to take part, while others were uncontactable.

WHAT'S IN A NAME?

What makes a gin a "Lancashire" "Cheshire" "Lake District" "Liverpool" or "Manchester" gin? Is it using ingredients from the place? Or water from one of its springs? Is it making the base spirit from scratch on-site? Does the juniper need to be picked in the county? Does the distiller need to be born and bred there? Does the distillery have to be there?

The gin industry is not tightly tied up in rules and regulations, so there is no guidance on what might constitute a county or city gin. Where is the line to be drawn? Instinctively you might say a Lancashire gin is one "made in Lancashire", but that definition would rule out several names you would expect to be in a book about the county's gins.

To recognise the importance of the distillers who make their own gin,

I have used the classification I devised for *The GIN CLAN,* my book of Scottish gins and distilleries. Using Scottish terms, which I hope still ring bells in England, the entries appear under the headings "The Clan" and "Kith & Kin".

The Distilling Clan is the distilleries – its members have a still in the North West of England, and they use it to make gin.

The Kith & Kin are the rest: those we think of as North West gins. There are makers, creators and brand owners who have gin made for them in the region – and elsewhere. They could be makers who use compounding techniques to create "bathtub" gins. Some of the Kith & Kin plan on building their own distilleries, so will graduate to the Clan in due course.

The classification is not perfect, but it is a neat reflection of the gin scene in 2022. And to be clear, this is a book about gin – full-strength gin.

THE TASTE OF JUNIPER

In the European Union, the minimum bottled strength for "distilled gin" and "gin" is 37.5% ABV (alcohol by volume). This book concentrates on those gins. There are also "juniper-flavoured spirit drinks" – including

Dutch jenever or genever – with their own rules and bottled at a minimum of 30% ABV. And many fruit liqueurs – some marketed as fruit gins – but below 37.5% ABV.

The EU defines "distilled gin" as one made by redistilling alcohol of agricultural origin with an initial strength of 96% ABV in stills traditionally used for gin in the presence of juniper berries and other natural botanicals. The juniper taste must be predominant. London gin and London Dry gin are types of distilled gin with nothing added after distillation apart from water.

Alongside that is "gin", a juniper-flavoured spirit drink produced by flavouring neutral alcohol of agricultural origin with juniper berries and other natural substances. Again the taste must predominantly be that of juniper. This includes what is referred to as "compound" or "bathtub" gin. In each definition, there is the stipulation for gin to have a "juniper-led" flavour.

As makers become more and more adventurous in their choice of botanicals, the juniper flavour can almost disappear, and, as many point out, if you leave out the juniper it is just a flavoured vodka. Compared to Scotch whisky, which has more than a century of tight regulation, gin has very light rules and plenty of scope for innovative interpretation. And many people are loath to dampen that spirit of creativity. The debate around juniper will continue.

Another area of concern is that you see the word "gin" used on products that are obviously not gin. There have even been non-alcoholic brands launched which make a play of being "not gin". And liqueurs can often make much of the gin part of their brand, although they contain very little gin and are bottled at well below 37.5% ABV.

All this might not matter to the consumer if they enjoy what they are drinking, but some makers are concerned about the potential damage to the reputation of their premium product.

TOASTING THE FUTURE

One trend that has been emerging over the past few years is the focus on sustainability and the environment. Many makers were keen to point out to me their green credentials. There is no doubt that distilling can be harsh on the environment – water and energy are key to the process but makers are introducing green measures where they can. It might be removing plastic from packaging, choosing lighter bottles made from recycled glass, or finding practical uses for spent botanicals. There are examples of solar power and some quite inventive ways to reuse water cooling the still.

Those foraging their botanicals talk about harvesting in an ethical and sustainable way and some are planting and growing their own ingredients. What is interesting is that I could only identify two grain-to-glass distilleries. Forgan takes grain grown in fields within a few miles of its stills in west Lancashire. Pip Robbins then makes his own neutral grain spirit – something which most distilleries buy in. Weetwood in Cheshire also makes its own spirit from barley mashed in its own brewhouse before creating its gins with it.

THE GIN DRINKERS

Making gin and putting it into bottles is never going to be a success without the consumers ... and getting a maker's message out to the marketplace is rarely done without help.

The retailers and bar staff which promote gins are an important part of the picture. In Manchester, the Atlas Bar has become a beacon for gin with approaching 600 bottles in stock, while the Old Bell Inn at Saddleworth in Lancashire has more than 1,500 gins behind the bar – and an entry into the Guinness World Records. Plenty of farm shops and stores have impressive walls of gin, with Chestnut House at Pooley Bridge beside Ullswater in the Lake District typical of a business run by a knowledgeable team who promote the gins of the area.

Cocktails are a key part of the vibrant nightlife in Manchester and Liverpool, and they drive the interest in premium gins – particularly among the bartenders who make them. The fashion for flavoured gins has also brought new fans to the gin world. Like cocktails they also make stunning social media posts. And what town doesn't have a gin bar – or at least a pub – which promotes its local gins?

Then, there are restaurants and hotels who are working with makers to create their own house gins. Goosnargh Gin has worked with Mark Birchall, chef-patron of Moor Hall, the two Michelin starred restaurant at Aughton, while Sandgrown Spirits collaborated with Lisa Goodwin-Allen, the two-star Michelin executive chef at Northcote in the Ribble Valley. Then there is the chef who liked the gin so much that he joined the company, with TV presenter Simon Rimmer joining Tappers in the Wirral.

Distillers also make the most of talking directly to the public. Meeting a gin's maker is one of the joys of exploring the gin world. We are often

Herdwick Distillery

lucky enough to meet them at festivals and markets as we "taste before we buy". Some welcome visitors to their distilleries and share their secrets – a few will even help you make your own gin. Planning a holiday around distilleries with an open door can make a very pleasant itinerary with Cheshire and the Lake District good places to start.

WHO MAKES IT?

Gin might have largely gone out of fashion in the 20th century, but James Bond and Gordon's kept it in the public consciousness. People became more interested in gin again as they found Bombay Sapphire in the 1990s and, when the premium gins such as Hendrick's and

Tanqueray No Ten were launched as the new century dawned, there was a renewed appetite for the old favourite, especially in cocktails.

When legislation changed in 2008 and allowed smaller stills, the artisan or craft ginmakers stepped up, led by Sipsmith, the architect of the rule change. At the end of this century's first decade, whiskymakers were also testing the water. The Botanist, Caorunn and Edinburgh Gin came from companies with established whisky brands.

The first modern gin with roots in the North West appeared in 2005 when Whitley Neill Gin was launched by Johnny Neill, a descendant of the Greenall family who took over Thomas Dakin's Warrington distillery. In Cumbria, Bedrock Gin was launched in 2008. But it was 2013-14 before gins really started to appear from the North West. It was 2014 which welcomed the first gins from three of the area's best known names – Batch, Forest and the Lakes Distillery.

The ginmakers are from all walks of life: from agriculture, hospitality and IT to teaching, the police and marketing – there is no pigeon-holing a ginmaker. Reasons to make gin are as numerous as the entries in this book. The dreams of the makers are what fuels much of the modern gin boom.

There are the farmers looking to diversify their livelihood, the entrepreneurs wanting to celebrate their beautiful home town and the gin enthusiasts who wanted to have a go themselves. There are some solely focused on gin, a number who are producing gin as a step to making whisky and those who are making it alongside beer and other drinks, including tonics. For some, making gin is the purely commercial addition of a brand to a portfolio of drinks.

Whatever the reason, it all adds up to the overall picture of gin selling like the proverbial hot cakes. We might ask if it will last. Gins from artisan makers certainly grew the market in the early 2010s. Further growth has been because of the popularity of pink and flavoured gin. Data for 2018 showed that flavoured gin had driven more than half the growth in gin, despite only making up one-fifth of total sales. We have witnessed a stream of flavours launched although not all last long. Vodka is also getting in on the act, with *The Grocer* magazine reporting in June 2022 that increased sales of flavoured vodka in supermarkets have been at the expense of gin.

Will gin continue to be the flavour of the month? Some say the next trend will be savoury gins, others point to flavoured rum and vodka … or perhaps absinthe or mezcal. For now, let's raise a glass and toast the makers of gin in Cumbria, Lancashire, Cheshire, Liverpool and Manchester.

THE
DISTILLING CLAN

Clan (a tribe or collection of families subject to a single chieftain, commonly bearing the same surname and supposed to have a common ancestor)

These are the gin distillers of Cumbria, Lancashire, Cheshire and the cities of Manchester and Liverpool. They have a physical still in these places where they make gin. They may also make other spirits – there are several whisky distilleries, as well as makers of rum, absinthe, vodka and liqueurs. In some cases, they make gin for other brand owners under contract, or they may allow "cuckoo distillers" to use their stills to make gin.

The distilleries are listed by their name or company's name – not necessarily the name of the gin.

THE ANCOATS DISTILLERY
[Ancoats Gin]

Ancoats, Manchester
ancoatsdistillery.co.uk
First gin: December 2019

The cobbled streets and converted textile mills of northern Manchester are a melting pot of cultures and history. Investment and regeneration means Ancoats is now an edgy, arty and vibrant neighbourhood. Inspired by the plump blackberries thriving beside a derelict pub which seemed to capture the rebirth of Ancoats, Peter Ramsay has developed a distinct, funky, modern gin for the area.

Ancoats Blackberry gin has 14 botanicals including orange and lemon. A London Dry-style gin, the berries are steeped in the spirit first. Working with another city distiller, Peter had been learning the gin-making process so that one day he would be able to make his gins in Ancoats himself.

For their second gin, they made organic raspberries their hero fruit and then adapted the original recipe again for a non-berry Signature Gin with orange and lemon, peppercorns, Sichuan pepper, cardamom and celery among its 13 botanicals. To cater for drinkers who prefer a more traditional style, they have also created Ancoats Classic Gin.

Peter's ambition to set up his own distillery came true in the summer of 2022 when he installed a 50-litre copper still with a gas heater from Portugal in an industrial unit in Ancoats.

An artist and craftworker, Peter, who taught at a school in the area, gives us a visual tour with his bottle designs. The Ancoats logo is based on the archway above the entrance to the Ancoats Dispensary, a landmark red brick hospital building which is being transformed into residential apartments. The bee is styled to be a bit wasp-like to give the Manchester worker bee more attitude.

The Signature Gin features the Guardian of Ancoats, a bird mural (now erased) by Mexican artist Mateus Bailon. The Ancoats range, which includes vodka and rum and comes in ceramic bottles from Germany, features other street art, including work by the Spanish duo PichiAvo on the Classic Gin. Painted on Port Street in 2016, *The Conflict* depicted Hercules in battle with Nessus, but was covered up a couple of years later.

BATCH DISTILLERY
[Batch Signature, Industrial Strength, Lime Leaf, Buddha's Hand]

Burnley, Lancashire
batchdistillery.co.uk
First gin: November 2014

Adventure lies at the heart of Batch. From the first days starting out as a "gypsy brewer" Phil Whitwell has explored flavours. In 2012, his taste for the unusual led to the nascent gin scene and quickly he applied for distillers' licences at his Hampshire base.

It took a year of learning and experimentation to come up with the first gin. The breakthrough was when an online botanical shop's Christmas-time recommendations included frankincense and myrrh. Phil ordered some and they are now the hero ingredients of Batch Signature Gin.

Phil, who has a background in IT, soon realised that the South East of England already had plenty of ginmakers, so Batch moved north. Burnley is near to Phil's sister and there was plenty of support – from the council and his nephew, Ollie Sanderson, who ultimately became a distiller too. In 2014, based in the basement of a terraced house in the town, Batch was the first gin on the Lancashire scene.

By constantly innovating, Batch has been on an adventure ever since. The second gin Whinberry was inspired close to home with the berries picked in the area in the early autumn, while others originated further afield. Buddha's Hand was inspired by a trip Phil made to Shanghai where he tried the oddly shaped citrus fruit. Garam Masala Gin is an exploration of Indian ingredients, while Cloud Forest uses Costa Rican botanicals.

The Batch team has looked to other spirits for ideas. Ginavit is a juniper take on the Scandinavian spirit, aquavit, while Gin Rummy is a series of barrel-aged gins. Batch has also made whisky and botanical blends which do not have juniper.

As head distiller Ollie was devising many of the recipes until his decision to change career in 2022. Bottled at 55% ABV, his Batch Industrial Strength is a bold reference to the industrial heritage of Burnley. His mantle has been taken on by Ryan Evans, who started out with Batch as an apprentice. Phil still keeps his hand in.

The imaginative gins flow out of the former cotton mill,

which Batch moved to in 2016. There is Ramona, the 500-litre still which is used for the biggest selling gins and Adrian, a 165-litre still for the shorter-run Innovations Club gins, which appear monthly.

Producing new gins so frequently is possible because Batch has its own label printing machine and has the talents of graphic designer, Jane Griffiths, and artist, Bodie Cameron, to call on. This gives Batch the flexibility to fill its distinctive bottles with a succession of limited editions. The bespoke bottles which are fluted, have a B on the collar and a rose on the base, are made by Allied Glass in Yorkshire. They are sent out to customers – both individuals and retailers – and exported to the United States.

Future adventures are likely to see additional premises and, of course, additions to the Innovations Club.

BIG BANG BREWERY
[Gravity Gin, Lemon & Allspice
Dry Gin]

New Brighton, Wirral
www.bigbangbrewery.co.uk
Launched: March 2019

Pushing the boundaries is nothing new for ginmakers, but two scientists in the Wirral clearly have another world in their sights as they create their spirits. Laboratory analysts Ant Ryan and David Maloney used their experience in the pharmaceutical industry to observe the reactions of ingredients as they developed recipes for their Gravity Gins.

Their launch pad was the colour-changing properties of certain ingredients. Their Pear & Berries Gin unusually starts as green, rather than blue, and changes to shades of pink/purple depending on the mixer. Made by the compounding method, it is infused with 12 botanicals and uses blue butterfly pea flower for the natural colour change. It stands beside Ginger & Citrus gin which glitters in the light.

Alongside their obvious interest in out-of-this-world gins, the pair are keen to protect their own world and are sourcing community-grown botanicals, as well as offering a deposit-return bottle scheme.

Having quit their jobs to form Column Craft in 2020, they have added to their line-up with a first distilled dry gin – Lemon & Allspice – launched in 2022.

Since they moved from Ant's front room to their distillery, an eclectic, quirky, cool space which is a former supermarket store room, they have room for three (one 40-litre alembic copper and two 50-litre steel) stills. They also have a Taproom bar.

And they have been busy launching other drinks. There is Relativity Rum and a botanical spirit without juniper called Vlabc (because it uses vanilla, lemon, alcohol, beer hops and cardamom). They are also brewing their own Wirral Squirrel beer.

BIG HILL DISTILLERY
[Spirit of George, Rose Gin]

Mobberley, Cheshire
bighilldistillery.com
First gin: December 2017

In the race to conquer Everest, the highest mountain in the world, we often overlook the men who pioneered the challenge – finally achieved by Sir Edmund Hillary in 1953. George Mallory was one of the early mountaineers who set off to reach the 29,031ft peak. On his 1924 expedition he might even have succeeded but he was last seen alive 800ft from the summit. Nobody had been higher at that time.

Mallory came from Mobberley, and for village residents David Clayton and Ben Kaberry his fighting spirit is inspiring. In 2016, the pair, conscious of the growing interest in craft gin, started on their own adventure. After 18 months of learning and recipe development, they launched the Spirit of George from their distillery in the heart of the village.

In Mallory's honour, there are Himalayan botanicals in the London Dry gin. An organic wheat neutral grain spirit is steeped with the botanical blend before being distilled in a bespoke handmade 130-litre copper pot still with a gas burner, named Ruth. Some botanicals are vapour infused during distillation.

David and Ben work with Fairtrade farmers in Nepal to source the ginger, cloves, cinnamon, cardamom and the subtle Himalayan tea which contributes to the overall smoothness of the gin. In fact, Mallory has been such an inspiration that they went to Nepal themselves in May 2022 and trekked to Everest Base Camp – with a bottle of Spirit of George, of course.

In gin terms, their second challenge was to create a pink gin. With no added sweeteners or sugar, Rose Gin is delicate, with notes of raspberry, mint and vanilla from its nine botanicals. Like the Spirit of St George, David and Ben bottle and label Rose Gin themselves, while holding down full-time jobs. The labels bear close inspection as the barcodes reflect the date of Mallory's climb (08061924). There are also images of the Nepalese botanicals hidden in the drawings.

In the summer of 2022 they started to convert an old barn nearby, giving them more space for their business. The distillery is also increasingly the scene of collaborations, creating gins for other people. These include Camino, Cholmondeley Arms, Dexter & Jones' Rufus and Suburban Green gins and a special edition for Fortnum & Mason, the London store.

BLACK POWDER GIN COMPANY
[Sidelock, Flintlock, Fireball Chilli]

Weeton, Lancashire
blackpowdergin.co.uk
First gin: July 2017

From a farm steeped in history comes an explosion of gins. John Loftus and Tony Dalnus took the inspiration for their distillery name from the tradition of the Royal Navy testing the strength of gin by mixing it with gunpowder. The fact that the distillery is close to an Army barracks only adds to the picture.

John, whose family has farmed at Preese Hall Farm for more than a century, has turned a quest to create a perfect sloe gin into a thriving business making fruit gins and liqueurs. His son-in-law Tony concentrated on creating their signature London Dry gin – Sidelock – infused with 28 botanicals including rose petals, hibiscus, chamomile, grains of paradise and cranberries. Also in his sights was the Navy strength Flintlock which, with a powerful juniper streak, hits its mark at 60% ABV. Tony, whose background is in drama education, uses a traditional copper pot still, called Horatio.

The farm known for breeding world-class cattle, is the source of many of the fruits for John's creations. Since they set up the business, they have planted more than 150,000 trees and moved the stills from their original space in a barn to a purpose-built distillery beside the lake where they run dinner, drinks and live music experiences and private events.

They have also been busy developing their Severed Hand Rum brand, as well as making whisky and bourbon, meaning Black Powder has a catalogue of about 40 products. They created Tangerine Gin for Blackpool Football Club which sees sweet-scented tangerines infused in Sidelock. And there is the range of full-strength fruit gins featuring flavours such as English Quince, Lancashire Rhubarb, Amalfi Lemon and Cucumber & Rose. Meanwhile, Fireball comes with a safety warning for its explosion of chilli in a full-strength gin.

BRIMSTAGE DISTILLERY
[Brimstage Gin]

Upton, Wirral
www.wirralginschool.com
First gin: June 2019

Bog myrtle once grew profusely on the Wirral Peninsula. In fact, the area was called Myrtle Corner – or WirHeal in Old English. When Eric Healing set up his small craft gin distillery in Brimstage, a village right at the centre of the peninsula, he wanted to ground it in the community.

He was no stranger to gin, having launched Wirral Gin in 2015, and was keen to get back to his roots and work on a small scale. Using a traditional method, making really small batches, Eric's focus is on producing a fine gin in limited quantities at the distillery-come-gin-school which moved to Upton in 2022.

The signature gin is a London Dry and it is that bog myrtle that gives it a floral nose which is followed by a lingering spice. Other full-strength gins in the range feature flavours such as Raspberry, Japanese Watermelon, Brazilian Orange or Blackcurrant & Liquorice.

Eric, who has a background in IT, uses nothing bigger than a 30-litre all-copper still and, being such a fan of the metal, has called his company Copper Star. It also operates the Friday Night Gin Club, tastings and runs classes as the Wirral Gin School.

BRINDLE DISTILLERY
[Cuckoo Signature, Solace, Sunshine, Supernova, Sloedown]

Brindle, Lancashire
www.brindledistillery.co.uk
First gin: June 2017

Legend has it that the people of Brindle tried to prevent the first cuckoo of spring from leaving their rural village by building a wall around its field. They hoped that if it stayed so would the sunshine which ripened the harvest, but the plan failed and people born and bred in the village are still known as "Brindle cuckoos".

They might be third-generation Brindle folk, but the Singleton family have set their own cuckoo free in the gin world. When beef farmer, Gerard Singleton, realised that neither he nor his children saw their future solely in agriculture, he set about diversifying into the production of gin.

A cowshed is now a distillery and Cuckoo gins have been flying off the 100-acre farm. The first Cuckoo was a London Dry-style gin which has citrus, cinnamon and coriander notes. For Sunshine, lemon peel and vanilla take on elderflower and chamomile in the still before it is compounded with raspberries and honey from hives on the farm. When you add tonic it turns pink.

A modern Spiced Gin was created by head distiller, Mark Long, who is also Gerard's son-in-law. Bursting with spice, it is mellowed by jasmine, fig, rosehips and tonka beans before a burst of orange. Using his experience in the food industry, Mark has developed Cuckoo's other gins – plus rum, vodka and, in the long term, whisky.

With fresh water from a spring on the land, power from a biomass boiler and animals hungry for gin's by-products, a sustainable approach to the environment was obvious. When they came to change their bottles, Gerard and Mark turned to Allied Glass in Yorkshire for a bespoke design which is made from recycled glass and is 50 per cent lighter, neatly cutting their carbon footprint. The familiar screen-printed illustrations by Dorothy Charnley on the original labels have been incorporated into the glass, alongside embossed lettering and a curved shape which reflects their surroundings.

Home-grown and sustainably sourced botanicals are a feature of the gins they make on Maggie, the German 400-litre copper column hybrid still, named after Gerard's great aunt. The still is at the heart of the distillery which has become a tourist destination in its own right with its gin-making workshops and tours, alongside the Cuckoo's Nest, the distillery bar and events space.

Farming is very much rooted in the community and when illness hit Mark's wife Liz, everyone from medics to friends rallied round. Swift treatment was key and to thank people for their help – and to support those who might be going through the same thing – they created Solace. The juniper-rich citrus gin has savoury notes from olives, rosemary and lemon thyme and raises money for Jo's Cervical Cancer Trust.

CALENTILLO SPIRITS
[Rushcart Gin]

Strinesdale, Lancashire
www.calentillo-spirits.com
First gin: October 2019

The tradition of the Saddleworth Rushcart dates back to the Middle Ages when rushes were taken to the villages for use as floor coverings. Celebrations evolved around the arrival of the carts. The modern take sees Morris Men converge on Saddleworth to dance and pull a cart piled with rushes around the villages. For Chris and Amanda Moat this colourful event was inspiration for a range of gins.

Rushcart Gin has the classic botanicals of juniper, coriander, angelica and orris root, with oats added for smoothness and sweetness. Whinberry, Citrus and St Clements line up in the London Dry range. Raspberry, Cranberry & Orange, Rhubarb & Ginger editions add fruit and sweetness from handmade syrups to the Rushcart core gin.

Another tradition sparked the idea of distilling for Chris and Amanda. In Italy, they had flavoured alcohol-soaked sugar cubes – zuccherini alcolici – after a meal. Finding the alcohol in the supermarket they took some home, planning to recreate the sweet treats but, like many holiday souvenirs, it lay untouched. It was not until they visited the City of Manchester Distillery that they realised their Italian alcohol was neutral grain spirit (NGS) and the basis for gin so they started experimenting.

Soon they found that to buy more NGS was difficult without being a licensed distiller but they realised it was something they wanted to do after careers in financial services. Plenty of learning, experimenting and planning followed before they launched their business. First called Kin Spirits, they felt Calentillo better suited their style. It comes from the Spanish calentar "to heat" and they hope their products will add a little warmth to people's lives and special occasions.

They set up the distillery in an annex where their copper alembic stills – a 20-litre and a 40-litre – are kept busy. Having launched in 2019, all was going well until Covid and they had to rethink their business model, which had been aimed at creating bespoke spirit drinks for bars, restaurants and events. They pivoted to online sales and introduced cocktail-making classes and kits. Life might have returned to the pre-pandemic ways of working with clients, but the cocktails live on.

CHESHIRE DISTILLERY
[Kuro, Capesthorne Gin]

Siddington, Cheshire
cheshiredistillery.com
First gin: July 2017

The distillery on the Capesthorne estate is the culmination of a long journey for Craig Fell. It can be traced back to his student days working in bars, through his career in design to launching Kuro gin in 2017. In 2020, Craig took the keys of the former barn on the estate deep in the Cheshire countryside and, after renovations, it is now home to both the distillery and his branding and design agency.

Kuro had been inspired by a skiing holiday in Japan and it features bamboo leaf, silver birch bark and spruce needles among its 12 botanicals which also include nutmeg, cinnamon, orange and lemon. Initially distilled under contract, and then by Craig at other people's distilleries, it is now made at Capesthorne for both home and international markets. Kuro's siblings – Haru Blossom and Natsu Peach – also capture the essence of Japan, while the dramatic branding calls on Craig's design expertise, honed in bringing spirits to market for clients.

At the heart of the Capesthorne operation is a 400-litre hybrid still, named Penelope after one of the estate owner's ancestors. Penelope Ward was born in 1700 and died, aged 37, having had 11 children.

To mark the founding of his own distillery Craig has created a range of Capesthorne gins. The Classic Cheshire Dry has aromas of orange and lemon, prominent juniper flavours with woody undertones and a long

pepper finish. This stands beside two gins which capture the essence of the British countryside – Raspberry & Blueberry and Rhubarb & Lavender.

The distillery also allows Craig, who although self-taught had the support of one of the industry's most experienced distillers in his spirits education, space for further projects. There are flavour ideas to expand the Kuro family and the possibility of other spirits to explore. He also hopes to use the distillery space and tasting bar, with small intimate events possibly on the cards.

CITY OF MANCHESTER DISTILLERY
[Three Rivers Gin]

Manchester
cityofmanchesterdistillery.com
First gin: July 2016

The alchemy of gin revealed behind the unremarkable facade of a Manchester railway arch has captivated countless visitors to the City of Manchester Distillery since it opened in 2016. As a pioneer of the gin experience, it quickly became a favourite tourist destination. Today a visit is a rare privilege as tours have been scaled right back.

Home to Three Rivers Gin, the distillery was created by Dave Rigby who at the time owned a bar, having been a university lecturer in film studies. His interest in gin had grown with owning a bar and through meeting the co-founders of Warner's Distillery in Northamptonshire and distilling consultant Jamie Baxter who became a mentor. With little money, Dave and his father worked on transforming the arch into a distillery for more than a year, driven by vision of a home for a gin worthy of the name of the city.

The industrial area which grew up around the three rivers – Irwell, Irk and Medlock – of Manchester had to be at the heart of the brand. Dave wanted to create a gin that was progressive and inclusive and to demystify the ginmaking process. When the distillery opened to the public, it was one of the first to offer gin experiences where visitors were introduced to the city's industrial heritage, the history of gin, the process of making it and the Three Rivers story, before creating their own bottle of gin.

Pride of place at the Red Bank Parade distillery is the 450-litre Holstein copper pot still, Angel, named after the nearby Angel Meadow. Here Three Rivers is made with 11 botanicals which include oats – a staple in the diet of the city's workers in the industrial revolution. The balanced but complex London Dry gin has citrus, sweetness from vanilla, cinnamon and almond and spiciness from cardamom and black pepper.

With the success of Three Rivers, Dave's reputation as a distiller meant people approached him to make gin for them. As the list of clients grew, Dave in 2020 launched Alcohol Solutions, a company which creates, produces and packages beverages for a wide range of businesses. At Carrington, about 10 miles from the distillery, it has a development laboratory, bond, canning and bottling lines and a capacity to process 10 million cans and bottles a year. The City of Manchester Distillery and

Three Rivers Gin are part of Alcohol Solutions.

Three Rivers Gin has been joined by Manchester's first legally-produced rum and, in the summer of 2022, the city's first whisky came off the still. Dave is still hands-on with distilling and product development, but has help from Brandon Baker, a distilling graduate of Heriot-Watt University in Edinburgh.

CUMBRIA DISTILLING CO
[Cumbria Distilling Co Gin, Carlisle Gin]

Carlisle, Cumbria
www.cumbriadistilling.co
First gin: March 2018

Cumbria Distilling Co is a brand new beginning for Paul and Becky Carruthers, but they are in fact gin veterans. Having moved back home to Carlisle in 2019, they have now consolidated their operations under the Cumbria name.

Nurse Paul and midwife Becky first created a gin in their kitchen distillery in Manchester. The floral London Dry Fenney Street Gin was inspired by an old country foraging book they had found at Paul's grandfather's farm in Cumbria. A wildflower cordial recipe led to the inclusion of rose petals, elderflower and lavender along with spring water from home. It soon became a popular drink across the city.

On trips home, the pair realised that their birthplace was crying out for its own gin, so they created Carlisle Gin. The Signature London Dry is a simple five-botanical classically juniper-forward gin and they use it as a base for their fruit follow-ups. The striking labels include familiar sights around the city and are drawn by local artist Yvette Earl.

Paul, who still works in healthcare, makes the gin in a small practical space on the edge of Carlisle, where his faithful bespoke 250-litre still is set to be upgraded as demand grows. In the future they hope to create a distillery in Carlisle where they would have space for tastings, tours and workshops.

Launched in the summer of 2022, Cumbria Distilling Co Gin has three expressions, Signature, Blood Orange & Lime and Raspberry & Passionfruit. Again at its heart is a classic juniper-forward gin. Future Cumbria gins will be developed in partnership with a mixologist to make sure they work for the on-trade and because they are what the drinkers are asking for. There are ready-to-drink G&T cans and a vodka in the pipeline. The striking branding comes from Cann Creative in York.

DEFIANCE DISTILLERY

[Defiance Premium, Wild Rose, Old Tom, Navy Strength]

Oldham, Lancashire
www.defiancedistillery.co.uk
First gin: September 2017

Food and drink have been important passions in Paul Sheerin's life. They run through the globe trotting of his 20s, opening a delicatessen and studying for his Wine & Spirit Education Trust diploma. It was while writing his dissertation for his diploma that he met the team at Batch in Burnley and became hooked on gin. He went on to learn the secrets of distilling at Batch.

When he founded his own distillery, his approach to creating gins focused on using what nature offers on his doorstep. His first gin, Defiance Premium, features Sitka tips foraged at Whalley in Lancashire, and sweet flag (or tangerine root) and sweet cicely from Yorkshire. The foraged botanicals, which are collected only when they are in season, are steeped overnight before being vapour infused with another 13 botanicals. The gin is the base for Defiance Strawberry and Wild Rose gins, as well as the Old Tom, which features birch tree syrup from the Pennines. In 2020, Defiance Navy Strength was named best in category at the San Francisco World Spirits Competition.

In the distillery, a 250-litre reflux still takes centre stage. She is named after the Tolkien character Galadriel, the Lady of the Woods, which ties with Paul's foraging. The distillery is where Paul can be found developing further drinks both for Defiance and for clients, such as Atlas Bar and Edison Bar in Manchester, C&O Wines in Timperley and consultant chef Michael Harrison. Launched in 2019, there is Flight Club, a range of gins, rums and liqueurs inspired by Nick Harrison, a Lancashire designer who specialises in aircraft, and themed around military aeroplanes.

There are also Vintage Gins where the bottles celebrate the year and the decade and some unusual toffee vodkas. The distillery is home to a weekend bar where customers are encouraged to BYOV (bring your own vinyl) and the Gin Academy where you can create your own bottle of gin.

THE EDGE DISTILLERY

[The Edge, L'orange, Pear, Fruits of the Forest]

Astbury, Cheshire
theedgegin.co.uk
First gin: October 2018

What do you do when you have spent 18 years travelling the world? Make gin was the answer for cruise ship entertainers Clare and Michael Ryan. Inspired by a well in the woodlands of the Edge, the escarpment close to their home in Alderley Edge, they set off on a journey of discovery in the world of gin.

An inscription on the well set them thinking about the magic of creating gin. It also introduced them to the legend of the wizard and his band of warriors who are sleeping in a chamber below ground, ready to awake in a time of crisis to save the country. Locals believe the wizard is Merlin and the warriors King Arthur and his Knights of the Round Table.

On their quest, Clare and Michael headed to Lancashire to learn about ginmaking from friends in Oldham and then set up their own distillery in an industrial unit at Congleton. They finally found a home for their four stills – named Merlin, Arthur, Guinevere and Lancelot – at Alcumlow Hall Farm in the village of Astbury in 2021. The distillery – which has had former incarnations as a pilates studio and a pottery – is open to the public with tours, a bar and shop.

Their signature gin is The Edge, a London Dry style which uses ten botanicals including dried lemon and orange peel and their hero ingredient goji or wolfberries. The berries give a natural sweetness to the crisp complex gin. The fruits and zest are pre-soaked in the spirit for 24 hours before being vapour infused in the 25-litre column head stills which have stainless steel bases and copper columns.

The Edge stands beside three full-strength fruit gins – L'orange, Pear, and Fruits of the Forest. None have sugar added and all use the signature gin as their base. With a pair of The Edge vodkas already, look out for a Navy strength gin which is due to launch in 2022. All are presented in smart black bottles – or refill pouches – with flashes of colour on the labels to reflect their flavours. Of course, there is a wizard working his magic on the design.

EMERALD GIN
[Emerald Gin, Pink, Navy Strength]

Heald Green, Cheshire
emeraldgin.com
First gin: December 2020

Photo: Alex Boyd

Gareth Ball and Scott Grayson used the first Covid lockdown well: they built a distillery. They had started their company in September 2019, having been on a practical distillery course and gained all their licences and permissions before Covid struck in 2020, so they used the time to construct the shed in Gareth's garden that is now their distillery.

The initial dream of making gin had come to them on a beach holiday with their wives – twin sisters, Danielle and Charlotte. Making the idea reality was not made easy by the fact they both have full-time jobs: Gareth is an operational firefighter and Scott an airport warehouse operative.

Their signature London Dry gin was initially devised on a 2.5-litre copper alembic pot still and they now use a 100-litre Genio still, named Olivia after the Valencian beach where they first had the idea of making gin. It is juniper led with strong, citrusy flavours mixed with delicate floral notes and a fierce, spicy undertone.

It was followed by a Pink Gin made from the London Dry base combined with fresh strawberries, lime peel and pink peppercorns. A 57% Navy strength is again based on the original recipe, but with added juniper and citrus for punch. Like the distillery they – and a joiner friend Glynn Newlove – built, the gin is all hand-bottled and dressed with smart jewel-inspired labels designed by graphic artist Kate Booth.

Not prepared to sit on their laurels, they have been working on further recipes. They hope that by resting their signature gin in a 200-litre American oak ex-bourbon cask it will take on its smoky flavours. The barrel is from White Peak Distillery in the Peak District which they had visited on their distillery course. In the meantime, there is a Dark Berry gin with blackberry, raspberry and blueberry flavours to perfect and a Valencian Orange gin to craft in honour of making their Spanish beach dream come true.

FAITH & SONS
[Original, Mango, Cold Press Coffee, Raspberry & Rosehip]

Trafford Park, Manchester
faithandsons.co.uk
First gin: February 2016

Filipe Sousa's Original gin recalls his home city of Lisbon. Its six organic botanicals include lemon verbena which grew at his childhood home and mandarins which his grandmother bought for him. It was a leap of faith that took Filipe from bartending in Portugal to making gin in England. Having decided he wanted to make drinks rather than pour them, he learned about the process with distillation expert Dr Klaus Hagmann in the Black Forest in Germany.

Taking the name Faith & Sons – in recognition of his change in circumstances – Filipe started making gin in his Manchester kitchen, then moved to a garden shed before taking the keys to his Trafford Park unit in January 2019. There he does all the distilling – using copper still and rotavap – preparation and aftercare with help from his assistant, Jack Foster, and his own wife, Maria.

Filipe pays great attention to detail, so when mandarins are in season they are imported from Sicily for him to prepare and the lemon verbena is grown in his own garden. His most ambitious creation is probably his Cold Press Coffee Gin bottled at 38% ABV. The green coffee beans sourced from Guatemala are roasted and then cold pressed at the distillery before being rested for up to 24 hours and blended with Faith & Sons gin.

Felipe's talents are in such demand that he has created gins for other people, as well as his own range of liqueurs and those under the No Name Distillery brand. He might be well known for his juniper spirits, but Filipe admits his ambition was never only to "do" gin. He has already made rum and vodka and says that we should expect tequila and ultimately whisky.

THE FOREST DISTILLERY
[Forest Gin, Earl Grey]

Macclesfield, Cheshire
theforestdistillery.com
First gin: December 2014

The Forest Distillery story begins on a kitchen table at the home of Karl and Lindsay Bond close to the Macclesfield Forest. With their daughter, Harriet, they found ingredients in the forest and became amateur home distillers. Quickly the IT products trader and beautician realised that they were on to something and they tried selling their gin and ultimately set up in business.

The Forest gin distillery is a 17th-century stone barn surrounded by nature and the woodlands of the Peak District National Park. They use organic juniper, coriander, angelica, liquorice root, vanilla pods, along with foraged wild bilberries, raspberries and blackberries, moss, ferns, gorse flowers, spruce and pine, grinding the foraged botanicals by hand using a pestle and mortar. They use 25-litre copper stills, with the resulting spirit blended with water from a spring in the forest.

Earl Grey Forest Gin is distilled in the same way as the signature London Dry gin, but oolong tea from Chester blender Quinteassential, bergamot and cornflowers are infused into it. The gin is a rich, dark colour with delicate notes of Earl Grey tea.

Both gins are presented in porcelain bottles designed especially for Forest Distillery by Wade Ceramics in Stoke-on-Trent, Staffordshire. The artwork is by the Hertfordshire papercut artist, Suzy Taylor, who based it on the ingredients in the gin. She also created the brand's weasel, which is a native inhabitant of Macclesfield Forest.

In 2020, with Forest's whisky making gaining pace, the grain still was moved to a nearby coaching inn, the Cat & Fiddle, which at 1,689ft above sea level makes it the UK's highest whisky distillery. Forest now also operates the Little Shop & Bar in Buxton, Derbyshire, and a 2022 collaboration has put Forest to First Gin on Avanti West Coast Trains.

FORGAN DISTILLERY
[Forgan 42, Raspberry & Lavender]

Banks, Lancashire
forgandistillery.com
First gin: October 2017

Forgan is one of those rare finds – a golden nugget in the gin world – a grain-to-glass distillery. Pip Robbins creates alcohol from scratch using grain grown within a few miles of his stills. It means that his gin takes time to make. He ferments grain, mineral water, sugar and yeast for up to 10 days and lets the spirit settle. Only then does he start the triple distillation process to make the Forgan 42 gin with its light citrus and earthy notes and hint of spice from cardamom and pink peppercorns. Forgan's 74% and 80% ABV editions come with more intensity. In Forgan Raspberry & Lavender, Pip takes his Signature 42 and infuses it with the organic hero ingredients for a dark gin with a big fruit burst and slight hint of lavender.

The path to the Forgan Distillery is also a long one. Having become fascinated by gin and its science, Pip spent a year applying for a full distiller's licence which allows him to create alcohol from scratch instead of buying it in. Leaving behind a career which has spanned gold mining, heavy engineering and IT, he created his distillery, using a family name which dates back to 1625 and has roots in Scotland.

By being able to make his own spirit, Pip is also able to craft other drinks, such as Bourbon-style corn whisky and rum, with the same control and attention to detail. Forgan 48 100% Corn Spirit is made from grain that grows in the field next to the distillery. Here, in an "unremarkable" space, Pip runs three stills, two 50-litre matching reflux stills, named Michelle after his wife and Lisa after her twin sister, and a 300-litre column still, named Elena after his neice.

G&J DISTILLERS
[Greenall's, Bloom, Opihr,
Thomas Dakin, Berkeley Square]

Warrington, Cheshire
quintessentialbrands.com
First gin: 1761

Each year 61 million bottles of gin start life in an industrial estate on the outskirts of Warrington, close to the junction of the M6 and M62 motorways. G&J Distillers, part of Quintessential Brands since 2011, is one of the UK's biggest players in the gin market, but the Birchwood site is no soulless factory. At its heart is Master Distiller Joanne Moore. When she became Master Distiller in 2006, the company's gins were selling well, but there was a gap in the market for premium products. Joanne developed a gin flavour wheel and targeted the floral notes for her first gin, Bloom, in 2008. Berkeley Square quickly followed in the herbaceous space, while Opihr (launched in 2013) is spiced and Thomas Dakin (2015) is savoury.

In the late 18th century it was a Warrington distiller, Thomas Dakin, who pioneered the London Dry method for ginmaking. After the Greenall family took over his distillery and brewery, the Greenall name was applied to his gin recipe, making it the oldest gin in the UK. Joanne, the guardian of the recipe for Greenall's Original, has created its fruity editions which include flavours such as Wild Berry, Black Cherry and Blood Orange & Fig.

The operation has come a long way since Dakin bought land in Warrington's Bridge Street for his distillery. By the 1930s there was a huge distillery at Loushers Lane, opposite the Greenall Whitley brewery. In 2005, a devastating fire razed most of the site, with just the stills

escaping. With major customers to keep supplied, all the stops were pulled out to restart production after only ten days. Within three years G&J was operating at a new location at Birchwood.

Today the site has two still rooms, three bottling lines – capable of filling up to 500 bottles a minute – and warehouse space as far as the eye can see. One of Quintessential Brands' four production sites in Europe, it has about 170 employees and a keen eye on its carbon footprint which means it operates a zero waste-to-landfill policy and a range of resource-saving measures.

Alongside the company's own brands, the site makes gins for a long list of clients – from the UK's major supermarkets and international retailers to well-known brands and small individual organisations. At the Spirit Centre, clients can partner with G&J to create a drink tailored to their own requirements. They can work with Joanne and her team on flavour profiles, call on market insight and consult a library of bottles, stoppers and labels for their bespoke gin, which G&J would then make.

GINSMITH MANCHESTER
[Prosecco & Blood Orange, Prosecco & Raspberry Premium Gins]

Bacup, Lancashire
www.ginsmith.co.uk
First gin: December 2020

What goes into a still is a world away from what comes out. It was a lesson that Phil and Rebecca Smith learned quickly when they decided to start making gin. The couple had a long-held passion for gin and many friends across the industry, but no hands-on experience of ginmaking.

Among those friends, Dave and Ang Gandy owned a successful mobile gin bar and together they discussed the idea of producing a gin for the bar. Phil liked the idea and, as he had friends at Defiance in Oldham, he set about learning everything he could about gin and running a successful distillery. Defiance founder, Paul Sheerin, is now his consultant.

It was during the Covid lockdown that Phil and Rebecca were creating their distillation room and navigating red tape to obtain bank accounts and the necessary licences, but eventually they were ready to go. Phil, who has a background in engineering and sales, and Rebecca, a teacher, knew what the final style of gin should be, but getting there was the lesson they had to learn. They spent months experimenting – trying out distillation, maceration, steeping, double distillation and bathtub techniques – and creating recipes to find the right balance of fruit and botanicals.

With five versions to choose from, it was time for the Gandys to taste the results and decide on the Premium Gin for their Bee-Ginning brand. Using a 25-litre column still, named Mavis after Rebecca's aunt, the chosen recipe has 19 botanicals. Blueberries are steeped for 48 hours in neutral grain spirit before the botanicals are added. Subtle fruitiness comes from blueberries, blackcurrants, cranberries and homegrown black sambuca berries, while pink peppercorn, cassia, bitter orange peel, pink grapefruit, seabed coconut and almond combine for a smooth refreshing gin.

Alongside Bee-Ginning Premium Gin, the Gandys now have Queen Bee Navy Strength, a range of flavours – from Cool Cucumber to Champagne & Strawberry – and a selection of Manchester-themed gins.

Phil has also created gins for his Ginsmith Manchester label and Prosecco & Blood Orange, Prosecco & Raspberry, Blueberry & Blackcurrant Premium Gins are available, in bottles sealed with wax and stamped with his clever GS logo.

THE GINSMITHS OF LIVERPOOL

[Ginsmiths of Liverpool Dry, Merchant Navy, Marshmallow, Love Lane Gins]

Liverpool
lovelanebrewery.com
First gin: December 2017

The gins from the Ginsmiths of Liverpool are rooted in the heritage of their home city. The Liverpool Dry Gin is infused with sea holly, the official flower of Liverpool. It is a rarely used botanical that grows in the sand dunes along the coast and it is picked each summer. With almonds it creates a luxurious mouthfeel, while pink peppercorns add warmth to the citrus notes of lemon and orange peel and the earthy sweetness of liquorice.

The Merchant Navy Gin honours the busy port of the 1700s when exotic herbs and spices were arriving from the New World. It features yuzu peel, Australian pepperberry and Mexican vanilla for an intense gin bottled at 51% ABV.

Overseeing operations is gin veteran John O'Dowd, creator of the city's first gin in 2013. Having sold Liverpool Gin to Halewood International in 2016, he turned his attention to a new distillery.

The Ginsmiths of Liverpool is part of Higsons 1780, a company founded by Stephen Crawley. Having been the managing director at the Caledonian Brewery in Edinburgh, Stephen returned home to Merseyside in 2013, his heart set on establishing a brewery in Liverpool. He revived the Higson's brand which dates back to 1780 and whose beers had been an integral part of Liverpool life for 200 years.

Stephen then bought the Liverpool Craft Beer Company, with its Love Lane ales. This opened up the opportunity to transform an old red-brick rubber factory in the Baltic Triangle into a brewery and distillery, which is where John comes in as master ginsmith.

The work began on the site in 2016 with the Love Lane Brewery Bar and Kitchen and the Ginsmiths' distillery the result. Next to the brewery, which is capable of making more than 2.5 million pints a year, the distillery is home to a 150-litre still which is visible to guests in the bar. It is also the focus of tours and the gin school.

Although the Ginsmiths of Liverpool steeps itself in tradition, it also innovates as its Marshmallow Gin illustrates. This gin's hero is marshmallow root, as used for medicinal purposes by Liverpool's

Chinese community, which when dried has a heady vanilla, saccharine nose. The gin – a modern take on an Old Tom – was developed by one of the Ginsmiths team, Ben Murphy, a distilling graduate of Heriot-Watt University in Edinburgh, who has gone on to become head distiller at the Ad Gefrin whisky distillery in Northumberland.

Since 2018, Love Lane Gins have been targeting the trend for flavours. Often only found behind the brewery bar, editions have included Pomegranate Pink and Passion Flower. John's creativity also saw a ground-breaking collaboration with Glenfarclas whisky where a gin was designed to harmonise flavours as it matured in a first-fill Glenfarclas cask on Speyside. It had such good feedback that it would not be a surprise to see it return in the future.

GOOSNARGH GIN
[Goosnargh Gins' Chapters]

Whitechapel, Lancashire
goosnarghgin.co.uk
First gin: October 2018

One of the surprising things about the Forest of Bowland is that its fells, valleys and moors are not better known. The area in north-east Lancashire is designated as an Area of Outstanding Natural Beauty, has become a hub for artisan food producers and is well within reach of the county's big towns and cities, yet it is often overlooked by tourists.

Less surprising is the way Goosnargh Gin makes the most of its home in the Forest of Bowland. The small family distillery makes no secret of the fact it celebrates its surroundings. Not only are its gins designed around those surroundings but the founders, Richard and Rachel Trenchard, work with local artisans and independent businesses as much as possible. Inspired by Richard's background in journalism, their gins come in chapters, each telling its own story.

Their contemporary Signature gin – Chapter One – has 14 organic botanicals including meadowsweet, yarrow and elderflower, chosen to capture the spirit of the fells and meadows on their doorstep. Chapter Two celebrates the forest's Dark Skies Festival in a delicately spicy gin which is perfect for stargazing with its notes from aniseed, root ginger, cardamom and vanilla. Further Chapters are similarly inspired by the nature around them. And there is a collaboration with Mark Birchall, chef-patron of Moor Hall, the two-star Michelin restaurant with rooms at Aughton.

The labels for their apothecary style bottles were designed by Pete Sharp of March Design Studio and inspired by the roe deer which trot past the distillery. Limited edition stoneware bottles, hand-thrown by master potter Dylan Cross in Poulton, also feature the graceful animal.

All the gins are created in their distillery, a building which at one time served as the village post office and cafe. It is home to a Canadian 120-litre copper pot still, called Bea, which replaced their original 60-litre still which was destroyed in a fire in 2020. The small space is where they do everything – from preparing botanicals to bottling and packing – and host their intimate gin schools and foraging days. In 2021, a visit by TV cooks, the Hairy Bikers, Si King and Dave Myers, showcased the area, putting Goosnargh Gin on the map for a wider audience.

HALEWOOD ARTISANAL SPIRITS
[Liverpool Gin, JJ Whitley, Whitley Neill]

Chorley and Liverpool
halewood-int.com
First gin: August 2005

Halewood has become one of the major names in the UK gin sector – and it has strong roots in the North West. Not only is the family from Cheshire, but it owns gins which have links back to the pioneers of the modern gin industry.

Founded in 1978, when Wallasey-born John Halewood created a company selling Bulgarian wines, the firm now has more than a dozen brands including Whitley Neill Gin, Liverpool Gin, JJ Whitley Vodka and Gin, Dead Man's Fingers Rum, Crabbie Whisky and Gin, Samuel Gelston's Irish Whiskey and Hawkshead Brewery. At the helm is John's widow, Judy, as chairman and Stewart Hainsworth as chief executive. It is responsible for many thousands of litres of white spirits – gin and vodka – a year.

Halewood operates three distilleries in the North West. Liverpool Gin has its own distillery in the city centre, while a site at Chorley in Lancashire makes a range of white spirits and the Bankhall Distillery in Blackpool makes bourbon-inspired whisky. The Chorley site also has a major bottling plant and facilities to produce branded and own-label spirits, liqueurs and cocktails for clients.

The gin heritage goes back through the Whitley family. In 2009, Halewood bought Whitley Neill Gin from Johnny Neill, who founded it in 2005. Although the gin now has a home at the City of London Distillery, the Neill family's involvement in Merseyside distilling can be traced back to Johnny's great-grandfather, John James "JJ" Whitley, who was managing director of Greenall Whitley & Co and G&J Greenall, the Warrington distiller, until 1942. JJ's grandmother, Isabella, was also a descendant of the distillery's 18th-century owner, Thomas Greenall.

Launched in 2016, JJ Whitley Handcrafted Gins and Vodkas were originally produced in Chorley, before moving to the St Petersburg Distillery in Russia. Since the conflict in Ukraine in 2022 production has returned to Chorley. The imaginative flavours of the gins are inspired by JJ who developed a curiosity for wild vegetation as a child when he spent days exploring the gardens and hedgerows around his home in Daresbury.

The London Dry Gin is a classic recipe, which has eight botanicals, including orange and lemon peels, juniper, angelica seeds, coriander seed, liquorice, cassia bark and orris root. Flavours such as Pink Cherry, Blood Orange, Mango & Papaya, Strawberry Bramble and Violet make a colourful sight in their embossed bottles.

Halewood bought Liverpool Gin in 2016 and, having initially made it at its Sovereign Distillery in Huyton, opened its own dedicated distillery, bar and gin school in Castle Street in 2018.

HANDMADE GIN COMPANY

[Anfield Gin, Everton Gin, Tipsy Tortoise, Bakewell Gin]

Birkenhead, Wirral
handmadegin.com
First gin: October 2015

One of the most prolific ginmakers on Merseyside is the Handmade Gin Company. In its portfolio in the summer of 2022 there were 37 gins, 26 gin liqueurs plus a catalogue of more than 150 bespoke gins made for other companies. They celebrate the places and flavours of the area. There are gins for Crosby, famous Liverpool locations and the city's Everyman Theatre, while Bakewell Gin captures the cherry and almond cake flavours of the teatime treat.

It all started when Peter Golightly, a long-standing fan of gin, thought he would try making gin himself. With a copper still and appropriate licences he started to experiment with recipes, enjoying his results privately with friends until he hit on the hero ingredients of lemon and ginger. Inspired by the gingerbread-making history of his Lancashire home town, Ormskirk Gin went on sale in 2015. By 2017, the former corporate IT executive had launched the Handmade Gin Company.

As befits a busy operation, Handmade is now based in a large warehouse where several small copper alembic stills are used to create the large number of individual products. In charge is Claire Barclay who uses her experience in the police to manage the batches of gin through the stills, into bottles and out to the drinkers.

Again it was a quirk of fate that brought Claire to making gin. In 2017, after a career which took her from the beat to undercover, firearms, protection and community roles, she and her husband, Richard, were enjoying her retirement. Among their hobbies was gin and one day Claire was tagged on social media for an advert for "an apprentice distiller". She chuckled at the thought and sent the distillery a message, thinking nothing more of it ... but Claire joined Handmade the next week.

She quickly had the place running more efficiently and was soon distilling and creating her own ideas. The flavoured gin craze had started and she and Peter set to work on retro flavours such as black jack, dandelion & burdock and Parma violet. Their Violetta shimmer gin put them in the spotlight when the glittering spirit went viral on social media. Handmade's own gins include Marshmallow, Shimmering Strawberry Candyfloss and a Navy Strength edition.

Claire also developed the bespoke side of the business, creating gins for numerous organisations from charities to events. Scouse Bird gins were created for blogger and influencer Steph Johnson and her popular Scouse Bird shop in Liverpool. Packed with attitude – and flavour – the range started with a pink gin featuring rose, grapefruit zest and subtle spice and has blossomed into Mango & Passionfruit, Lychee & Lavender, a London Dry and vodkas.

HATTERS DISTILLERY
[Hatters Gin]

Stockport, Cheshire
hattersdistillery.com
First gin: April 2018

There was a time when the Cheshire town of Stockport was making 50,000 hats a week. No surprise to see that the town's football team is fondly called the Hatters. No surprise either when Stockport son, Sacha Mannion, set up a gin distillery in Edgeley near the Stockport County stadium, that he also named it Hatters.

A nod to the town was one of the things Sacha set out to achieve with his gin. He also wanted to create something his friends and family could enjoy that was fruity and packed with high quality juniper.

After he was granted a licence for his distillery in September 2017, it took him seven months of experimentation to come up with his 14-botanical recipe. However, the son of pub landlords, Sacha had a knowledgeable family who enjoyed helping him in the process.

The resulting recipe includes orange and lemon peels, three fruit berries, rose and elderflower. There is also honey from Steve Mead's hives in Mill Brow, Marple Bridge, east of the town. It means the sweet berries in Hatters Gin give way to the citrus, with subtle spice and a long fresh junipery finish.

Sacha, who works for a software company, makes the gin in a 25-litre electric stainless steel still with a copper head in his basement. Then he calls on the family for help in bottling, adding the distinctive blue wax seals and labels designed by Manchester tattoo artist, Jayne Rogers.

He also produces bespoke gins for bars in Stockport and for one – Smoked Orange for the Cracked Actor – he smokes the botanicals for 12 hours before distillation. He is also lining up further editions for his own label. Expect Black Tea and Pink to join the signature Hatters Gin on the shelf, alongside other spirits in the future.

HERDWICK DISTILLERY
[Yan Gin, Marmalade Yan, Berry Yan]

Kendal, Cumbria
www.herdwickdistillery.co.uk
First gin: August 2021

If you are looking for local produce in Cumbria it won't be long before you come across products from Lakeland Artisan. Geoff and Mary Monkman have built a thriving business making jams, chutneys and sauces, as well as cordials, soft drinks and liqueurs. Brands such as Cumbrian Delights, Lakeland Liqueurs and Mawson's are firm favourites in shops across the Lake District.

When they found a spacious new unit to house their business on the outskirts of Kendal it was only time before they would want to make their own gin. Geoff, who has a background in hospitality and retail, went on a distilling course run by Jamie Baxter of Craft Distilling Services and set about developing recipes.

When the Monkmans picked up the keys to their unit it was March 2020 and the Covid pandemic turned life on its head. Undeterred, they created Herdwick Distillery beside their main production kitchen and bottling hall with a 300-litre stainless steel pot still called Doris (after Geoff's grandma) at its heart.

Their signature gin is called Yan after the way Cumbrian shepherds start to count their Herdwick sheep. Among its 10 botanicals, which include rosehip, cubis berry, ginger, orange and lemon peel, the stand-

out ingredient is sarsaparilla. It's a nod to the fact that they own soda-maker Mawson's and one of its heritage brands is Sarsaparilla cordial, the key ingredient in a traditional North West drink known as "sass n soda".

Having that soda-making capability, it was logical for Geoff to create Fell Tonic to pair with Yan. Made with water from the Cumbrian fells, lemongrass, citrus fruit zests, rosehips, cardamom pods and allspice berries, it is the way he prepares the cinchona bark which gives Fell Tonic its distinctive amber colour.

In the spring of 2022, Yan was joined by two colourful sister gins. Marmalade Yan takes the signature gin and blends it with marmalade syrup for a zesty citrus juniper flavour. Cranberries, strawberries, raspberries, redcurrants and blackcurrants give Berry Yan Gin a deep rich colour.

With the trio of gins presented in tall elegant bottles, it is no surprise that the same attention to detail has been put into creating a range of cocktail cans. Not content with the usual slick-sided cans, Geoff and Mary have sourced some with a tactile surface – ideal for picking up when ice cold. The line-up includes Yan with Fell Tonic and Berry Yan with pink lemonade.

It's a good thing the new production unit has plenty of space, because filling the cans is just one of the many tasks the Lakeland Artisan team does itself.

HOYLE BOTTOM SPIRITS
[Tinker Brook Gin]

Accrington, Lancashire
www.hoylebottomspirits.co.uk
First gin: March 2019

Creating gins has become a thriving business for brothers Jamie and Owen McNulty. The consultant distillers are kept busy with private clients who are seeking bespoke spirits that reflect their interests. It wasn't always so ... they launched their company Hoyle Bottom Spirits with their own gin, Tinker Brook a contemporary Lancashire Dry made with 12 botanicals including heather.

The gin's name comes from the river which turned the water wheel at Hoyle Bottom, an ancient cotton mill where their company was founded. The hand-foraged heather is a nod to Jamie's wife, Heather, who has since joined them in the business.

Today they offer clients a concept-to-glass service working with them on creating a drink and engaging branding, as well as handcrafting and packaging it at the distillery they moved to Accrington in the autumn of 2020. Their journey to contract distilling started years earlier when Jamie had come across "skittle vodka" while working as a rep in Spain. He developed an interest in distilling, researching and learning before buying a 20-litre still.

When, in 2018, he was looking for a change of direction from working in IT sales and travelling a lot, he set up the business with Owen, who was at the time teaching English in Spain. Owen, who moved back to Lancashire at the end of 2019, has a background in design and illustration which is now a key part of the service Hoyle Bottom Spirits offers.

Using a 200-litre hybrid stainless steel and copper still, called Roma, after the brothers' grandmother, they have already created a couple of dozen drinks, working with hospitality groups, bars and country estates. There have been full-strength gins for the Meanley estate in the Forest of Bowland and the Jane Eyre bar in Ancoats and a range of liqueurs for Albert's Schloss in Manchester, with more in the pipeline.

THE LAKES DISTILLERY
[The Lakes Gin, Pink Grapefruit Gin]

Setmurthy, Cumbria
www.lakesdistillery.com
First gin: June 2014

Breathing life back into a dilapidated Victorian dairy farm by building a new distillery took imagination, but for Paul Currie it seemed only natural. Paul, a whisky industry veteran, and Cumbrian entrepreneur, Nigel Mills, saw the potential and now the Lakes Distillery couldn't be further from the derelict site they first saw in the village close to Bassenthwaite Lake.

From the stunning modern gates to meticulously restored traditional stone and slate buildings, the distillery, bistro and visitor centre make a fitting addition to the National Park landscape. The main focus of the Lakes Distillery is whisky, with the innovative malts created by master blender Dhavall Gandhi receiving widespread praise as they challenge conventions. However, the gins came first and put the distillery, which opened in 2014, on the map.

The Lakes Classic Gin – updated by Dhavall in 2019 – now has vibrant notes of juniper, black pepper and orange peel. It is made by gently steeping nine botanicals in British wheat spirit, before a slow run through the traditional 1,000-litre copper pot still which is housed beside the whisky stills in a former barn. With pink grapefruit the suggested garnish for the Classic, the second gin adds the fruit for you so that all you need add to the Pink Grapefruit Gin is tonic. The gins line up beside a pair of gin liqueurs – Elderflower and Rhubarb & Rosehip – and vodka, and all come in elegant embossed bottles from Allied Glass in Yorkshire. The labels come from the James Cropper papermill in Kendal, a family business established in 1845, with the overall design inspired by the distillery itself.

During the distillery renovations, 26 carved quatrefoils were discovered in the stonework. These ancient Celtic symbols which represent faith, hope, luck and love, have been carefully restored and the quatrefoil has become the cornerstone of the Lakes brand. Part of its responsibility agenda means it takes a sustainable approach in its business, with waste products going to farms for fertiliser or feed, single-use plastic free waste, a borehole for water, a biomass boiler for the bistro and funding for local projects.

The distillery is also creating a modern artistic legacy. The gates which welcome its many visitors are by Cumbrian metalwork designer, Alan Dawson. They showcase the ingredients used by the distillery including wheat, barley, heather, hawthorn and, of course, juniper. The labels on the whisky bottles in the distillery shop are works of art in themselves, with specially commissioned designs for each edition.

LANCASHIRE GIN FAMILY
[Ramsbottom Gin, Rhubarb & Ginger, Once upon a Lime]

Ramsbottom, Lancashire
www.lancashireginfamily.com
First gin: October 2020

With time on their hands in the early days of the Covid pandemic in 2020, Jay and Cara Wilson turned their thoughts to creating a gin worthy of Lancashire. With Jay, a surveyor, on furlough, it was also setting a good example of taking the initiative for their children. With Jay's brother Mike they set about developing ideas, turned to experts for advice and before long the Lancashire Gin Family was in business.

The Ramsbottom Gin Signature edition uses handpicked whinberries among its ten botanicals for a London Dry-style gin and although the recipe was developed by them, early batches were made with Chris Moat at Calentillo Spirits in Saddleworth.

Jay and Cara have since set up their own distillery and in the summer of 2022 moved to a purpose-built garden annex. They have three alembic copper stills ranging from a 60-litre workhorse to their tiny test still called Bobby Peel, after the tower commemorating Bury-born British Prime Minister Sir Robert Peel, on Holcombe Hill. Their distillery sits at the foot of the hill and they have made its landmark tower a feature of their branding.

Using handpicked local produce where possible, Jay and Cara, who works in the retail sector, have created further Lancashire gins – Blackberry & Apple and Rhubarb & Ginger. All these gins are presented in bottles adorned with illustrations by Adam Rowlinson of Ramsbottom. They have also created gins to raise funds for Grace Kelly Childhood Cancer Trust and Sophie's Wish Fund. Sophie's Sparkle Raspberry Gin is sweeter and shimmers, while Once upon a Lime in Lancashire has a lemon and lime twist.

LIVERPOOL GIN DISTILLERY
[Liverpool Gin, Valencian Orange, Lemongrass & Ginger, Rose Petal]

Liverpool
liverpoolgindistillery.com
First gin: June 2013

Liverpool has been a gateway for exotic imports through the centuries and botanicals and spices were among the most precious cargoes landed. It is also a city that has a long-standing tradition of distilling spirits with two major whisky distilleries in Victorian times. So, as the 21st-century gin age took root, it was only time before the city would get its own gin. Liverpool Gin was the result of a conversation in 2012 between John O'Dowd and Mark Hensby who went on to launch it on International Gin Day in 2013. With intense juniper, coriander, angelica and citrus it is a well-balanced but complex gin.

Liverpool Gin was sold in 2016 to Halewood International who added it to its portfolio of premium spirits. Initially it was made at the Sovereign Distillery in Huyton, before the Liverpool Gin Distillery opened in Castle Street in 2018. The four-storey building houses not only the bespoke 600-litre modern copper version of a Carter Head still called Margaret, but also Bartender and Gin schools and bars. In charge is head distiller, Joe Hambleton.

The range of organic gins is inspired by the port city's exotic imports with oranges from Valencia and herbs and spices from Asia. The Valencian Orange Gin was created to celebrate John's son's wedding and welcome the bride using the fruit of her home town.

Lemongrass & Ginger Gin is built on the fruitiness of lemongrass and lime, with Asian spicy notes from fresh ginger, allspice and kaffir lime leaves. In contrast Liverpool Gin Rose Petal uses a secret blend of botanicals for a delicate romantic flavour. The bottles all bear the iconic Liver Bird, the mythical creature which is the symbol of the city.

LONG DOG GIN
[Long Dog Gin, Pink Strawberry]

Tottington, Lancashire
ginbylongdog.co.uk
First gin: May 2019

The idea of making gin struck Paul Coupe as he and his wife, Janette, were watching TV with their loyal red dachshunds on their laps. It was a bit of a bolt from the blue, but the fish and chip shop owner knew he wanted a new challenge.

Paul set about investigating the idea and found his way to the Batch Distillery in Burnley. There he spent time, learning from the team, working with distiller, Ollie Sanderson, to create a recipe and ultimately making his own gin. There was only one name for the gin – Long Dog – after the family pets, Max and Paddy. The London Dry recipe is based around their copper colour, using blood orange and red grapefruit in a juniper-heavy 15-botanical mix. Also making an appearance are ginger, lime, lemon balm, pomelo and rose and there are almonds for a smooth, creamy finish. To complete the product, the labels feature a copper-coloured dashhound design.

With Long Dog on the market, it was time to leave the Batch nest and stop being a "cuckoo distiller". In 2020, he moved to his own micro distillery with a 25-litre T500 still installed in his substantial garden shed. From there he launched Long Dog Strawberry Gin in the summer of 2022. It is similar to his signature recipe, but lighter on the citrus elements, with fresh strawberries macerated in the NGS before it is distilled. Afterwards Paul adds freeze-dried strawberries for natural colour and a tiny bit of sugar syrup and lemon. He bottles it at 38% ABV.

Paul, who has help in the distillery from Janette and his eldest son Kurt Titmass, hopes the next step for the family business, which goes by the name of Holcombe Gin, will be larger premises to accommodate his dream 300-litre still.

LUCKY BEE GIN COMPANY
[Lucky Bee Classic, Hench, TuttiFrutti]

Ashton-on-Mersey, Cheshire
www.luckybeegin.co.uk
First gin: October 2020

There is a lot of superstition around the number 13, but for Katy Moore and Stephen Appleby they have turned it into their lucky mascot. Katy, a fitness presenter, and Stephen, a rugby-playing IT consultant, use 13 different botanicals in their London Dry-style Lucky Bee Gin and they launched it on 13 October, 2020.

Their journey originated when they started exploring gin, having realised it could be low in calories and pure in nature which appealed to the health-conscious pair. A tour of the City of Manchester distillery kick-started their hobby, a course with Jamie Baxter of Craft Distilling Services crystallised their knowledge and by the March 2020 Covid lockdown they had obtained the licences they needed to set up a distillery.

They have since moved house and the distillery is now in a transformed outbuilding, complete with a mural by Sarah Lyall, with additional space in a garage. They use a 25-litre Turbo 500 still called Ned after Stephen's mother, with Pat, a three-litre copper pot test still, named after Katy's mother.

With the Manchester emblem of a bee in their brand, they have focused their attention on botanicals from the area. Both Lucky Bee's Classic Gin and the Hench Navy strength edition, have nettle and dock leaf foraged from the banks of the River Mersey and Manchester Ship Canal and silver birch from Priory Woods in Sale, alongside lemon and orange peels, cardamom and cinnamon. The Rhubarb Gin is distilled with produce from Timperley, where they lived before their move.

Having been drawn to 13 when so many would avoid it, Stephen and Katy want to teach people that it is OK to be different and not to fit in. Celebrating individuality and the Pride movement, they launched TuttiFrutti, a grapefruit and zesty lime gin inspired by one of Katy's favourite childhood sweets.

MURPHY'S DISTILLERY
[Murphy's Original]

Liverpool
www.murphys-gin.com
First gin: September 2019

Heritage runs strong in the Murphy family. Three brothers, great-grandchildren of Irish immigrants, have put it at the heart of their distillery in Liverpool's North Dock. The building is in sight of the Clarence Dock where many Irish immigrants like their relatives would have arrived on the boat from Ireland in the 19th century.

Ginmaking began as something of a hobby for Mark Murphy, who was a university biotechnology lecturer. He had taught plenty of students about distilling for the biopharmaceutical industry, but until he bought a 2.5-litre Portuguese still he had never made alcohol.

When Murphy's Original Gin received good feedback, Mark decided to give the business a go with his brothers, Simon and Terry. The gin is packed with botanicals giving it a robust and bold profile with citrus and peppery notes and it works well in cocktails or as a sipping gin. Murphy's fruit-flavoured gins still have a juniper core and they do not use sugar, artificial flavours or colours.

After Mark quit his job to work full time in the company and, as they navigated the pandemic, they moved from his kitchen into a former joinery at the docks. They converted it into a bar with space for their two 20-litre and two 40-litre Portuguese copper alembic stills. The smaller stills are named William and Bridget after their ancestors who left Wexford in 1889. As well as crafting gin for other people, Mark has launched a vodka.

Being environmentally conscious, the brothers have used reclaimed materials in fitting out the distillery and they have deliberately chosen bottles which do not use an excess of glass, paper labels and they compost their spent botanicals.

Although the Murphy brothers do much to celebrate their own heritage, they are also helping write the next chapter for the docks. With their popular bar and events, they are putting their mark on the area, at the same time that it is being regenerated by projects such as Everton's new football stadium, the Titanic Hotel and the Tobacco Warehouse apartments.

NO 1 FAIRHAM GIN
[Signature, Ochre Edition]

Penwortham, Lancashire
no1fairhamgin.com
First gin: April 2021

A craft gin which stood out from the crowd had been on the minds of Ellis McKeown and Liam Stemson for a while. It was Covid that gave them the time to develop the idea. Watched by their dog Bella, lockdown saw them buy a three-litre still and turn their outhouse into a distilling room. Together, with stubborn determination, they worked to develop a contemporary recipe around exotic fruits not commonly used in gins.

Calling on Ellis' background in marketing, they devised their branding around their village, the name coming from their home address. A year later their signature Lancashire Dry gin was ready to release. Its 13 botanicals create a juniper-forward base for the exotic fruits – guava, kumquat and physalis.

Before the launch they had moved to a small industrial unit and bought a 60-litre copper pot still, with a bespoke basket so that they could create their gins using vapour infusion. With Bella banned from the distillery, the still is named after her. The gin is not chill filtered so the natural oils and their flavours are retained. This means that when ice is added it creates a pearlescent haze.

The distillery has been set up to make as little impact on the environment as possible. For instance, they use bottles and packaging made from recycled material and their botanicals are ethically sourced. To counteract their inevitable impact, for every 70cl bottle sold they buy a sapling which will be planted by Ribble Rivers Trust across Lancashire.

Their second edition, Ochre is again strong on juniper, but is fresh from orange and sweet clementine and warmed with spices. Even though Ellis and Liam hold down full-time jobs, they do expect more editions to follow.

NO 186 GIN
[No 186 Signature, Berries & Honey, Passionfruit & Vanilla]

Manchester
www.186gin.co.uk
First gin: November 2019

Behind the mirrored door in the Manchester barbershop, lies a cocktail bar inspired by the late-night drinking dens of New York in the Roaring Twenties and prohibition era. Beneath a Grade II-listed building in Deansgate, One Eight Six has been a popular live music destination for gin drinkers since 2019 and it has its own gin. After a major refurbishment in 2022, it also has its own distillery.

No 186 Gin was developed by two of the bar's partners, Matt and Lynsey Postlethwaite, who are passionate about using local ingredients and suppliers. They worked with Lancashire distillery, Brindle, to create the gins, making sure they have no added sugars or artificial sweeteners. This choice was driven by the fact that when Matt was diagnosed with type 1 diabetes in 2013, he discovered gin as he looked to reduce his sugar intake.

No 186 Signature Gin is a smooth Mediterranean-style dry gin with a burst of citrus and grapefruit balanced by soft spice. Berries & Honey Gin teams vanilla with raspberries and natural honey from the Bee Centre in Chorley, while Passionfruit & Vanilla Gin is a take on the Pornstar Martini.

In 2022, with One Eight Six closed, Lynsey and Matt started producing the gins themselves on 20-litre stills while they waited for a 200-litre copper pot still to arrive. The bar has the still in view and there are tours and plans to develop other spirits.

In the distillery, Lynsey who had worked in social care, and Matt, who also runs a facilities management business, are conscious of their eco footprint and their coloured bottles, which are made and decorated in the UK, are reused wherever possible. In addition, for every bottle of gin purchased they donate 2,000 litres of clean water through the Water for Kids charity.

PENNINGTON SPIRITS
[Lakeland Moon Gin, Lakeland Moon Snowfell]

Kendal, Cumbria
www.penningtonspirits.com
First gin: December 2016

The road to Lakeland Moon Gin started with Kendal Mint Cake and Mike Pennington's success in creating a liqueur with it. He had grown up in the street where the sweet was first made and in 1990 he created the liqueur for Burgundy's, his wine bar in Kendal. It was only in 2015 that he started selling it – and his Bakewell Liqueur – to the public, which ultimately led to a flourishing spirits and liqueurs business and Mike selling the bar.

With the liqueurs selling well, Mike turned his attention to the idea of making gin. He recalled the juniper he found on childhood walks and how he loved the smell of the crushed berries. His partner, Annie Brownhill, found advice in the Old Farmer's Almanac which said that to capture juniper berries at their juiciest, most flavourful and aromatic, they must be harvested during the full moon.

And so Lakeland Moon Gin is made with juniper gathered from the Lakeland fells under a full moon and six other botanicals including grapefruit, Spanish orange and lemon peel. It is blended with water filtered through limestone beds from a spring in the Lake District National Park. Its sibling, Lakeland Moon Snowfell Gin, was created for the Craft Gin Club, and changes the balance of botanicals, introducing earthier, more herbaceous flavours into the blend, to transport the drinker to the snow-topped fells. Keeping it local, the Lakeland Moon labels are designed by Jonny Moss of Scratch Creative in Kendal.

Pennington Spirits has continued to expand and the range includes Lakeland Moon Rhubarb Gin Liqueur and Organic Vodka, as well as a Gingerbread Liqueur. In 2022, it moved into larger premises on the edge of Kendal. The distillery is home to a three-phase electric still which means Mike is making Lakeland Moon on his own equipment after five years of using kit belonging to another company. With the new site being in the National Park, Mike has designed the operation so that it runs off renewable energy, using a windmill and solar network with battery back up.

RIBBLE VALLEY GIN CO
[Little Lane, Country Market, Garden Party, Winter's Night]

Longridge, Lancashire
www.ribblevalleygin.co.uk
First gin: February 2019

Country Market Gin may well be the first vegetable patch-inspired gin. The use of tomatoes, carrots, shallots and beetroot in this contemporary gin alongside peppers, basil, pink peppercorns and wild thyme give it both savoury and sweet notes. It makes a G&T to go with cheese and biscuits.

It is one in a line-up of small batch gins created by Justine and Luke Moyes. Their distillery – a 19th-century stone outhouse which was once a piggery – is home to an 83-litre copper column still from Kentucky in which they slowly vapour infuse their gins. They use spring water which is rich in minerals from an estate in the Trough of Bowland.

The botanicals reflect their rural surroundings in the Ribble Valley and feature on the labels. Designed by Laura Brown of the nearby Shed on the Fell, each label showcases the botanicals in its gin. Justine and Luke started making gin as a hobby while working for the family packaging business. A visit in 2018 to the Salcombe Gin School in Devon set them off on their quest to showcase the countryside around their own home.

Ribble Valley's signature gin, Little Lane, combines heather, nettles, oak bark and meadowsweet, together with fresh blackberries and foraged pine. It is a leafy fresh smooth gin with floral notes and a gentle woody side.

There's a summer edition which celebrates the British garden. Garden Party Gin features strawberries, wild thyme, elderflower, rose petals and hibiscus for a fruity and floral finish. Meanwhile, Winter's Night combines peppery citrus with smoky black cardamom for a nights-by-the-fire gin.

Justine and Luke have also created gins for other organisations. Kingsman is made exclusively for the Duke of Lancaster's regiment to support soldiers, veterans and their families, which is a cause important to Luke, who served in the regiment. The gin commemorates its history and achievements with pine needles representing the Redcoats advancing through the pine forest in their assault on Quebec in 1759 and apple for the defence of La Haye Sainte orchard at Waterloo in 1815.

With the distillery established, Luke and Justine aim to create a space to host gin schools and pop-up gin nights and find time to make vodkas, rums and maybe even a whisky.

SANDGROWN SPIRITS
[Lytham Gin, Bee's Knees, The Navigator's, Positively Purple]

Lytham St Annes, Lancashire
www.sandgrownspirits.co.uk
First gin: April 2018

There is a little bit of Lancashire in every drop of Sandgrown's gins. And even the company name comes from the nickname – "Sandgrown'uns" – given to people from the Lancashire coast, which is very appropriate as Sara Dewhurst its co-founder is "as Sandgrown as they come".

Each of the gins contain something foraged or grown by Sara. In the original Lytham London Dry Gin it is the marsh samphire – or glasswort – which is responsibly picked on the shore of the Ribble Estuary close to Lytham's iconic windmill. It gives a silky mouthfeel to the 11-botanical gin with its zesty orange and spicy flavours.

Bee's Knees Old Tom Gin has a touch of honey from the Layton Bee Project in Blackpool with lavender from Sara's garden, pink peppercorns and a hint of lime. Sandgrown's Navy strength gin – The Navigator's – was created in memory of Sara's grandfather who was a Naval navigator during the Second World War. Distilled with apple juice and botanicals including lemon, rosemary, pink peppercorns, cardamom and cassia, it has herbaceous notes alongside a warm spice.

Positively Purple calls on Sara's past life as a chemist and science teacher and her knowledge of the natural colour-changing properties of some botanicals. Thai butterfly blue-pea flowers go from blue to lilac with the addition of a carbonated mixer. The dry and fruity gin brings together oranges and satsumas with an infusion of blueberries and blackberries from the local hedgerows. Sara makes her gins on a range of stills named after her grandmothers – strong women who lived on the Lancashire coast.

After 24 years in teaching, Sara bought a delicatessen and before long

was thinking about how to use her love of science and enhance what she sold at the deli. Gin was the answer as it combined her love of flavours, interest in molecules from plants and chemical processes perfectly. With Lytham's bar owners interested, and relevant licences in place, Sara and her husband Paul, who has expertise in food and drink manufacturing, set about creating a gin fit for their home town.

Originally located in her garage, the distillery soon moved to an industrial unit where she is now so busy that even her largest still – the 150-litre Elsie – is not really big enough. Alongside making her own spirits, much of Sara's time is taken up by distilling for other people.

She has created gins and rums for a number of businesses including Royal Lytham and St Annes Golf Club, Blackpool Pleasure Beach and Patwah Spirits. A high profile collaboration in 2022 was with Lisa Goodwin-Allen, the Michelin-starred executive chef at Northcote, the luxury hotel on the edge of the Forest of Bowland, to create Obsession Gin for its festival of Michelin-starred chefs.

SHED 1 DISTILLERY
[Cuckold's Revenge, Shed Loads of Love, Giggle in the Ginnel, Chilli Fest, Chuckleberry]

Ulverston, Cumbria
shed1distillery.com
First gin: October 2016

When Zoe and Andy met in South Korea in 2007 no-one would have predicted that they would now be running a successful craft distillery. For Andrew was an actor on tour with Shakespeare's Globe and Zoe an artist-turned-language-tutor working in Busan. The Arnold-Bennetts started the distillery in their garden shed after they had made their home in Ulverston and found that apples and foraged blackberries made a great compound gin elixir.

A licence from HMRC was the next step and soon they were making London Dry-style gins in their 7ft by 7ft shed. Their launch gins – Cuckold's Revenge, Giggle in the Ginnel and Festive Tipple – were quickly flying off the shelves.

Cuckold's Revenge which was actually their first gin, is classically distilled but contemporary in style featuring citrus and spice. Its name comes from Andy's last acting role as the cuckolded husband, Frost in Northern Broadsides' production of *Merry Wives*. Star anise is the signature botanical in Giggle in the Ginnel giving it a distinctive flavour enhanced by angelica, elderberry and fresh orange zest notes.

By 2019 they had out-grown Shed 1 and they took the keys of the Old Cow Shed at Ulverston's canal-side auction mart. They have transformed it into a charming quirky space where visitors can make their own gins, enjoy an afternoon G&Tea or even get married.

The teas are as inventive and attractive as the surroundings, with Zoe's edible treats matching the gins. A ramekin of baked yoghurt has a layer of chuckleberry jam and meadowsweet and hyssop crumble topping in a nod to the ingredients of Chuckleberry, Shed 1's first full-strength compound gin.

Behind the scenes there is a practical space for the still – a 100-litre stainless steel model with whisky cone and hood – and all the bottling, labelling, packaging and recipe development involved in a busy distillery. The still is called Yentl, after a character Andy's mother played when they acted together in his early 20s.

The distillery is where their care for the environment is evident. Andy has created a closed-loop cooling system which saves water being flushed away during distillation. There is also an "incredibly addictive" shredder which repurposes cardboard into packaging.

They support their community in many ways, most obviously in making lockdown sanitiser and with the Shed 1 Marmalade Fund. Zoe makes marmalade from the fresh fruit left after zest is removed for the gins. A donation from each jar goes into the charity fund.

SIS4ERS DISTILLERY
[Sis4ers Gin]

Salford, Manchester
sis4ersdistillery.com
First gin: February 2018

Salford is home to probably the world's largest alcoholic-making family. Eleven McAvoy siblings are either brewers or distillers. The men run the Seven Bro7hers Brewery, while the sisters make spirits. Lucy, who previously owned an events management company, ran the distillery for four years before her sisters, Kerry, Hayley and Kate left their teaching jobs to join her in 2021. Each of the four sisters has a dedicated role in the business.

They started out in a back room at their brothers' brewery before moving their distillery to its own space nearby. It is home to a 510-litre Arnold Holstein copper pot still, named Frederica after their parents Freda and Eric. It replaced a 200-litre copper column alembic still in 2021. Recipe development is carried out on the three-litre Arabella.

Sis4ers Signature Gin represents all four of the women, while the four infused, flavoured gins reflect their individual tastes and contrasting personalities. Signature is a classic blend of gin botanicals, with a hint of blueberry and citrus notes from orange and lemon. Lime & Thyme reflects the tastes of master distiller, Hayley, while Caramel Espresso Gin is dedicated to coffee fan Kate. Passion Fruit & Cardamom Gin comes from Lucy, while the Strawberry Edition is by Kerry.

They also make limited edition gins which included Home at Ten peach gin released during the pandemic to raise funds for hospitality charity, So Let's Talk. With the four sisters now working in the distillery, the business has been adding to its range with rum, vodka and ready-to-drink cans and they are busy welcoming visitors for tastings, experiences and afternoon tea.

SPIRIT OF GARSTANG
[Spirit of Garstang Lancashire Dry Gin]

Garstang, Lancashire
thespiritofgarstanggin.co.uk
First gin: October 2018

The Lancashire market town of Garstang has the honour of being the world's first ever Fair Trade town. Launched in 2001 to promote Fair Trade-certified goods available in the town, the idea has since spread around the world. On the High Street, Katie Harris has a bottle shop, Gin and Brews, where artisan spirits and local ales feature. It stocks Spirit of Garstang gins – with good reason because Katie is their maker.

Her distillery in a nearby village is an outbuilding where she has space for her 30-litre copper alembic stills – Steven, after her late father, James and Chris after her sons. The stills are all unique as she and her husband, a mechanical fitter, adapt everything to suit the way they like to operate.

After working with hundreds of distilleries through bar work, Katie wanted to make spirits with unique flavours that you could drink neat on ice, in cocktails or in a perfect serve. Having fun with flavours is part of the Spirit of Garstang experience. Alongside delicately spiced Lancashire Dry, Katie's first gins were Spiced Pear and Cucumber & Mint. The unusual flavour combinations have continued and the range includes Amaretto, Rhubarb Ripple, Spiced Zesty Orange, Black Raspberry, Mango & Passionfruit. Pink Citrus, meanwhile, has oriental influences and changes colour when a mixer is added.

Katie has formed a partnership with the Hooting Owl Distillery at Barmby Moor in Yorkshire for a range of Tipsy Toad spirits, where again fun is driving the flavours. She has also created rums to honour her highwayman ancestor, John "Swift Nick" Nevison, who in the 17th century held up travellers but was said never to use violence in robbing them.

SPIRIT OF KESWICK
[Sharp Edge, Striding Edge, Old Tom of Coniston]

Keswick, Cumbria
www.spiritofkeswick.co.uk
First gin: December 2018

The road to gin is not always direct. For James McIntyre it has taken him through time as a military bandsman, carer and retailer before arriving at a distillery in the heart of the busy Lake District town of Keswick.

James and his wife Jo have a quirky clothing brand called Sheep-ish and it was after they started selling Cumbrian craft beers in their shop that they thought they should sell some of the area's flavoured spirits as well. Rather than stock those that were already established and available in other stores, they decided to create their own.

After a lot of research, James and Jo launched their own liqueurs and ultimately made their own signature gin – now known as Striding Edge. It is vapour infused in Aimee, a T500 25-litre pot still with copper dome, with sage, rosemary, heather tips and lemongrass alongside more traditional gin botanicals.

Sharp Edge Gin is a more modern citrus-forward gin using fresh grapefruit, orange and lime peels with chamomile for balance. Old Tom of Coniston takes Striding Edge, cardamom and ginger and adds a post-distillation infusion of pink peppercorn syrup.

With a creative can-do attitude, James and Jo do most things themselves – from fitting out the shop to designing labels and printing or etching items. Although James is the main distiller, Jo is very much involved and can be found filling bottles, labelling, marketing, hosting visitors and being chief taster. They design their own branding and the gin's back label features a contour line illustration which shows through the bottle and captures the lakes and hills of the area.

For a couple who have rarely resisted an entrepreneurial opportunity, the one thing that is not on the agenda is making their spirits more widely available. They do not wholesale, so their products are only available on their website or in the distillery.

The full-strength Spirit of Keswick gins share the shop floor with liqueurs – which have an eclectic collection of flavours from salted caramel rum and toffee vodka to passion fruit, mango & elderflower gin – and their Cumbrian whisky liqueur, Hervyk. They also use the tails of their gin to make limoncello. With James and Jo's sprit of adventure, don't be surprised if there isn't another gin on the shelves soon.

SPIRIT OF MANCHESTER DISTILLERY
[Manchester Gin, Overboard, Wild Spirit, Tied the Knot]

Manchester
manchestergin.co.uk
First gin: May 2016

Romance is at the heart of the Spirit of Manchester Distillery – it was after the co-founders met in a bar and found a shared love of gin and tonic that the idea of creating a gin for Manchester took shape. Jen Wiggins and Seb Heeley started making gin on their dining room table before moving to Temperance Street and then to Watson Street where the Spirit of Manchester Distillery now sits beside their Three Little Words bar in the renovated railway arches.

They had set their hearts on creating a contemporary style gin and turned to dandelion and burdock root, a familiar sight along the city's waterways but also a traditional soft drink popular in the area. There are ten other botanicals including orange, lemon, liquorice and ground almond in Manchester Gin Signature.

Overboard, a Navy version of the Signature amplifies the citrus and intensifies the juniper. Wild Spirit introduces sage, thyme, orris, lemon balm and silver birch for a savoury take. There are also fruit – Raspberry or Blackberry – editions.

An ambitious 2021 launch was a collaboration with Michelin-starred Mana. Mother of Pearl Gin uses the Blossom Street restaurant's

discarded oyster shells alongside pine and lemon for a sophisticated seaside gin. Collaborations with Peter Hook, the co-founder of Joy Division and New Order, have celebrated the Haçienda, Manchester's iconic clubbing venue of the 1980s and 1990s.

Visitors can tour the distillery or try ginmaking sessions – all part of the "drink, dine and

distil" experience which is on offer at the Watson Street venues. At the heart of the distillery is Wonder Wend, a custom-built 1,000-litre still from China. Their original 60-litre copper still, Wendy – named after Jen's mother – is used for new product development. All the distilling takes place here, but an additional site was opened in 2021 to provide space for bottling, storage and shipping. The distillery has also extended its portfolio, with a range of flavoured botanical vodkas, One-Eyed Rebel rums, English vermouths and absinthe.

Proud to be part of Manchester, Seb and Jen adopted the bee in tribute to the city's work ethic and inclusive, hive mentality. And it reflects their approach to business which sees them use local suppliers, create jobs and launch apprenticeships in the community. They try to look after the environment and their striking custom-made bottle is now made from recycled glass with natural cork and wood heads. They also operate a refill scheme, have removed plastic from packaging, use motion sensor lighting to reduce electricity consumption and send zero waste to landfill.

And the romance continues. In 2022, after nine years together, Seb and Jen celebrated their own wedding with Tied the Knot, a limited edition gin in collaboration with the Craft Gin Club.

THE SPIRITUOUS DISTILLERY

[Spirituous Cool Blue, Elderflower, Wild Berry]

Thornton, Lancashire
spirituous.co.uk
First gin: July 2022

Put simply Spirituous means "alcoholic". With roots in Latin, French and old English it also means "laden with spirit" and is a fitting name for a distillery. It is also a good description of the Spirituous Distillery by the end of the Covid pandemic. Chris Cudlip had been gearing up to launch his distillery when coronavirus appeared and disrupted his bottle supply. So he got busy concocting new gins and other spirits to add to his signature Cool Blue Gin.

Cool Blue is based on a Dry gin and its botanicals are juniper, angelica root, cassia bark, coriander, cubeb, liquorice, orris root and grains of paradise by vapour infusion with citrus peel by post infusion. The result is a smooth citrus-style gin with complex aromatic spice notes and a touch of sweetness. The labels are inspired by the once common windmills of Lancashire's Fylde coast and his home town, Thornton, has one of the few well-preserved examples.

Originally an aerospace toolmaker, Chris has a long-standing interest in brewing and distilling probably fuelled by the amazing smells from the large brewery in Blackpool near his grandparents' home. The interest developed while working in California in the 1980s and then, fascinated by the rise of Sipsmith, the London distiller credited with launching the UK craft gin boom, he looked deeper into distilling by researching methods and equipment and taking training courses. Slowly the idea took root that he could make spirits himself.

By early 2020 he had licences from HMRC and Spirituous Cool Blue Gin was ready to go, but he had no bottles. So instead of selling his gin, he spent much of the pandemic in his kitchen distillery working on recipes using vapour infusion, maceration and concentrates from hydrodistillation. It meant that in the summer of 2022 he launched with three full-strength gins and various schnapps and liqueurs.

For now, the distillery is small and Chris is using two 25-litre electric stills, but he hopes to move to at least a 250-litre still next. He is also keen to utilise skills honed in the aerospace industry to embrace technology to reduce his carbon footprint in what is a power-hungry industry.

STABLE YARD DISTILLERY
[Stable Yard Classic, Navy Edition, Cloudy Lemon with Cardamon]

Goosnargh, Lancashire
stableyarddistillery.co.uk
First gin: December 2019

Using local ingredients added up for chartered accountant Sarah Shorrock when she decided to make gin. Sarah and Mark Sudell had been inspired to set up the business after visiting the Lakes Distillery in Cumbria. Sarah invested in Rosie, a 100-litre copper still, and spent the summer applying for licences and doing lots of research.

They were were keen to use ingredients from the countryside and the Classic Stable Yard Lancashire Dry Gin includes homegrown sliced apple, hawthorn berries and heather flowers. Sarah has infused the Classic with strawberry, raspberry leaves, orange, apple, sea buckthorn and hibiscus flowers for the pink Infused Wild Berry Gin. Cloudy Lemon with Cardamon Gin sees fresh and dried lemon with green cardamom pods added to the Classic.

Starting the distillery in a converted stable block on Bay Horse Lane, alongside Sarah's love of horses – she has two retired dressage horses – meant the company name was a given. The logo of two horses pulling a trap is based on a photograph of Mark's grandfather on the family farm close by. With the distillery now set up in Goosnargh, Sarah is planning to host private tastings and make-your-own-gin days.

STOCKPORT GIN
[Original, Twist of Lime, Bergara, Pink Grapefruit & Pink Peppercorn]

Stockport, Cheshire
www.stockport-gin.com
First gin: March 2019

Stockport has its own gin thanks to Paul and Cheryl Sharrocks. They loved to try the gins associated with the places they visited and realised that their home town was lacking one. A class at the City of Manchester Distillery opened their eyes to the possibility of creating one themselves.

It was not as easy as Paul, an architect, and Cheryl, a hairdresser, imagined and they had to immerse themselves in learning and experimenting before Stockport Gin could be launched in 2019. Vapour infused with lemon, orange and pine needles, it is a citrus-forward gin, with distinct notes of juniper and lots of earthy, foresty pine.

At first it was made in their garage but as the business grew and they had to convert their daughter's bedroom into a stockroom, they knew they needed more space. In July 2021, they set up a distillery in Stockport where they have not only production facilities, but also a shop and space to host distillery tours – and Paul has joined Cheryl in the business.

They use a 100-litre stainless steel column still to make their Original Gin and its siblings. Pink Edition is made with the Original's botanicals and then infused with strawberries, raspberries and pomegranates. Meanwhile Twist of Lime replaces the orange peel of the Original with fresh lime peel for a sharper, zestier taste. Their labels, designed by Sophie Ormsby, capture one of Stockport's most recognisable landmarks – the 27-arch viaduct which carries the railway over the River Mersey.

As Paul and Cheryl met at a Stockport County football match in Torquay in 2006, it's not surprising they have joined with supporters to raise money for a statue for Danny Bergara, the legendary manager who took the team to Wembley four times. Bergara Gin has botanicals from his homeland, Uruguay, such as feijoa (or pineapple guava), yellow passion fruit and yerba maté, a traditional herbal tea.

TAMESIDE DISTILLERY
[Tameside, Father's Ruin, Vitamin Sea, Willow Wood]

Denton, Manchester
www.tameside.net
First gin: December 2019

Once at the heart of the industrial revolution, Tameside – to the east of Manchester – is home to almost a quarter of a million people. It is now also home to a distillery revolutionising local drinking habits.

Lee Chisnall, a former IT professional, set up the distillery after extensive research into ginmaking, intent on creating high quality alcohol with authentic flavours.

His first product was the distillery's signature Tameside Gin which uses 24 botanicals for its balance of juniper, citrus, spice, herbal and floral flavours. He immediately went on to create Willow Wood Gin to support the nearby adult hospice in Ashton-under-Lyne. Four Berry Gin has since followed for the same cause.

Tameside's creativity continues with an interesting range of spirits taking shape. Recipe development makes good use of the array of modular stills which allows a variety of configurations for different spirits. Tameside Gin is a case in point with the 2022 release increasing the number of botanicals to 56, thanks to four separate distillations.

Vitamin Sea Gin, a Navy strength London Dry-style gin, is big on juniper, while Father's Ruin is a spiced, citrusy gin which uses 29 botanicals in its recipe. Full-strength fruit-infused gins line up beside spiced rums, all branded with a striking image of a bear – from an original drawing by the founder himself.

TAPPERS GIN
[Darkside Coastal, Brightside London Dry]

Upton, Wirral
www.tappersgin.com
First gin: May 2016

For Steve Tapril, proving that you could produce a good genuine local gin, is a matter of pride. He had been seduced into the world of craft gin as it developed at the end of the 2000s but had become disillusioned – and vocal – about the number of contract-made gins and manufactured backstories. He then decided to see what could actually be done and set about researching seaside botanicals that grew around his home on the Wirral Peninsula and perfecting his compounding technique.

After a year of experimenting, and a further six months of paperwork he was ready to launch the Darkside. The gin is cold compounded in stainless steel conical fermenters using foraged sea beet, chickweed and red clover, along with some traditional gin botanicals and lots of juniper. From infusing to bottling, the process takes about a week for a batch of up to 100 bottles.

The Darkside name is a nod to the rivalry between Liverpool and the Wirral. The smooth, rich and almost savoury amber gin in the Victorian apothecary-style bottles quickly gained fans on both sides of the Mersey. TV chef and presenter, Simon Rimmer, was one of them and he liked the brand so much that he joined the team in 2020. Launched in February 2020, Tappers Brightside Gin is the distilled version of Darkside.

The Tappers range includes limited-edition compound gins which each use the season's foraged botanicals. And there are intriguing specials – Hydropathic Pudding Fruit Cup, Figgy Pudding and Eggcentric Chocolate gins leading the way. Collaborations are a feature of the distillery and a limited-edition distilled gin, Dalglish 7, raised £19,520 for a cancer charity founded by Marina Dalglish, the wife of Liverpool Football Club legend Kenny. Tickled Pink Gin is a collab with Simon featuring Provence red rose petals and

hibiscus flowers and Tappers produced a 125th anniversary gin for the Royal Liverpool Golf Club.

Compounding is still a key activity at Tappers, but Steve has a 500-litre Holstein still called Lena, plus smaller traditional alembic pot stills. Having started out at home, he moved to an industrial unit, then, after securing a listing with Waitrose in 2021, it was time to move again and make a home for Lena.

The public were welcomed to the new Tappers Distillery and Gin School in June 2022 on World Gin Day. It hosts tours, make-your-own sessions and Thirsty Thursday open evenings. As the business grew, Steve had given up his university IT job to turn full-time distiller and his mother Sue joined him as finance and operations manager. He now has two distillery operatives who assist him in the production process.

TARSIER SPIRIT
[Tarsier Southeast Asian Dry, Oriental Pink, Taipei Old Tom, Khao San Gin]

Stockport, Cheshire
tarsierspirit.com
Launch: April 2017

Tarsiers, the tiny primates native to the Philippines give their name to these exotic gins. They are the creation of Tim Driver and Sherwin Acebuche who believe the large-eyed animals embody their vision of small-batch gins with big flavour and personality. After a backpacking trip around south-east Asia which introduced the pair to new cultures, places and cuisines, they decided to create a gin to celebrate the region's flavours.

First they had to learn about the ginmaking process and experiment with those flavours before they could launch Tarsier Southeast Asian Dry Gin from the back room of a pub near Manchester airport. They used two 60-litre copper alembic pot stills, named Florencia and Graciano after Sherwin's Filipino grandparents. It is a citrus-forward London Dry gin with aromatic and savoury mid-notes and a long peppery finish, the result of adding five signature botanicals to a traditional core.

Their hero, calamansi, a small green citrus fruit that combines the flavours of mandarin and lime, joins Thai sweet basil, galangal and Kampot red and black peppers to capture the essence of Asia. Calamansi and galangal also feature in Oriental Pink which sees them distilled

with dried raspberries, red dragon fruit (or pink pitaya) and seven traditional botanicals. The distillate is then infused with raspberry and lychee, for a light fruity gin with floral notes.

The gins are presented in bottles carrying an illustration by Juvel Tiu Modayno, a Filipino artist in Bacolod. Commissioned by Tim and Sherwin, it was hand-drawn in pencil before being transformed into a label. Since 2019, it has been screen printed directly on to the glass bottle.

In 2019, they moved to their own distillery in Stockport where they have a 500-litre iStill named Christian, after Sherwin's mentor. As many of Tarsier's gins are blended with distillates, they also cold distil using a vacuum still.

A series of backpacking gins take drinkers to far-flung places. Launched during the pandemic, Tim and Sherwin wanted people to be immersed in the destinations so you can scan a QR code on the bottle to share their experiences of the place. From their Taiwan visit comes Taipei Old Tom which balances the tea flavours from Oriental Beauty oolong with zesty kumquat, floral hibiscus and aromatic ginseng.

They have launched a collection of bottled cocktails, again inspired by their travels, so they have added a Filipino twist to a Negroni and a Thai take on a classic Bramble and there is a botanical spiced rum. Already exporting to more than 20 countries and planning to grow further, Tarsier supports its roots with 10 per cent of profits going to conservation projects in south-east Asia.

THREE WHEEL GIN COMPANY

[Trotter's London, Basil's Fawlty, Eric's Morecambe, Lancaster gins]

Morecambe, Lancashire
www.threewheelgin.co.uk
First gin: November 2019

Some things just make you smile and a three-wheeled Reliant Robin is one of them. Made a star in the TV series *Only Fools and Horses*, the Trotters' yellow van is very much a laughing matter – even 40 years after the comedy series first took to the road. Colin Scott, his daughter Catherine and her husband Peter Leonard have captured that sense of humour in their gins.

Their first was Trotter's London Gin because of their love for Del Boy and Rodney. As well as naming the company after their yellow van, Colin has restored one to promote the business. Next, the trio turned their attention to local talent with Eric's Morecambe Gin. Inspired by the classic breakfast sketch by Eric Morecambe and Ernie Wise, it is a "marmalade" gin using oranges, lemon and grapefruit. It also reflects the sunsets which regularly make a backdrop for Eric's statue on the town's promenade.

Fawlty Towers has a special resonance for Colin who is the chef-patron of the Blue Mountain Restaurant where their distillery is based. Basil's Fawlty gin is inspired by antics of the staff at the seaside hotel owned in the TV comedy by the hapless Basil

Fawlty. Thanks to basil and pink peppercorn, the gin has a little kick – not unlike the kick Basil would give to the waiter Manuel.

With the comedy gins on the market, the Three Wheel team created a range celebrating Lancashire's county town. Lancaster Pink is infused with raspberry and rose petals, while the signature is a classic Dry gin with lemon peel and buchu leaves, which are spicy but also evoke a mixture of rosemary and peppermint. Lancaster Blue is a colour-changing gin and a tribute to the NHS and keyworkers

of the 2020 pandemic. The Navy strength is Shields, first made privately for a family but now on general release.

It had taken about a year for the trio to set up their distillery, learning their craft and importing a still from Austria. The 50-litre stainless steel column still has copper bubble plates to improve the smoothness of the spirits during the vapour infusion.

There is a Lancaster Vodka, infused with locally roasted Kenyan coffee beans and vanilla and a popular Limoncello. They use only fresh fruit and have partnered with a Heysham juice company to use the peel left after making fruit drinks which is a neat solution for some potential waste.

THREE WRENS GIN
[Apple Crumble, Bison Grass, Bloody Apricot, Original Dry]

Combermere, Cheshire
threewrensgin.com
First gin: August 2019

Some dreams just have to be made to come true and for Nick Wadeson, his dream was to make gin. It took time – learning the craft, developing recipes and establishing a distillery – but now Nick makes gin in his own distillery. His imagination knows no bounds as he creates it and we have come to expect Three Wrens gins to have the hallmark of innovation. Juniper is at their heart, but he draws on his spirits industry experience, including his time as a Manchester mixologist, for unique flavour profiles. So, alongside a contemporary Three Wrens Original Dry Gin, we find world firsts such as Apple Crumble and Bison Grass gins.

Nick – and his assistant Fran Jones – take no shortcuts in producing the gins. For Bloody Apricot they spent a whole month hand-zesting blood oranges for the distillation, with toasted peel then steeped in the finished gin for a week. For the Apple Crumble, the oats are toasted and soaked in the wheat spirit for 48 hours. Nick seeks out exotic ingredients so that jara lemon, a bright green knobbly fruit from Bangladesh, and kumquat are the heroes of Exquisite Citrus Gin, launched in summer 2022. There was also a very limited release of a juniper-intense Navy strength, Three Wrens Legends, soon after.

The Cheshire countryside is also an important element in the Three Wrens story. The company name comes from Wrenbury, the rural village where Nick's family of three live. He first nurtured the brand in Cholmondeley, before moving in March 2022 to the Combermere estate. A one-time cattle shed houses production and packing operations, as well as a gin school. At the heart of the distillery are two copper pot stills – Valerie, Nick's 50-litre original, and her 300-litre sister with a deep vapour basket, called Jill. Nick also uses less traditional techniques, such as ultrasonic infusion, in developing his recipes.

Many of the botanicals are grown at the distillery including the rare bison grass which is more usually found in vodka. To secure supplies for Bison Grass Gin, Nick had to track down the seeds of the aromatic sweet grass from a botanist. As well as using home-grown botanicals, Three Wrens takes a sustainable approach with plastic-free packaging, tree planting, water recycling and a refill service for its bold bottles.

TURNCOAT DISTILLERY
[Turncoat London Dry, Cascade, Our Man in Sicily, Hold Fast]

Liverpool
www.turncoatdistillery.com
First gin: June 2017

The definition of a turncoat is a person who betrays or deserts one's principles. For Terry Langdon his principles were brewing but he was seduced by gin. He had recently sold the Liverpool Craft Brewery when a visit to the BrewDog distillery turned his head in the direction of gin. He and his science teacher wife, Jo, started to research and experiment in their garage in Kirkby.

They launched the distilling chapter of their lives with two gins – a London Dry and Cascade Gin. As a brewer, one of Terry's most successful creations had been Love Lane Pale Ale and its hero ingredient was Cascade hops, so he was determined to have a gin that connected him with his brewing roots. Developing it was not as simple as Terry expected, but it gave him and Jo valuable experience for the string of innovative gins they have gone on to create.

Among the 10 gins in the Turncoat portfolio, Our Man in Sicily is distilled with Sicilian lemons, while Dragon Tears is infused with the "dragon tear" leaf buds of jasmine and Bold St Chai uses a distillation of Chai Blend tea from the Leaf Tea Shop on Liverpool's Bold Street.

Bitter orange features in Hold Fast, a Navy Strength gin bottled at 60% ABV, while the seasonal edition for Botanical Garden in Liverpool's Baltic Triangle is loaded with orange peel and balanced by fennel leaf. River House Gin is a less expensive but tasty gin designed for use in a classic G&T or cocktail and there's a cost- and environment-conscious refill option.

Returning to Terry's roots, Turncoat has a "collusion" with Purity Brewing in Warwickshire, which uses hops from its own hopstore in an exclusive Cascade gin. Among other collaborations there is a gin due for MerseyMade, the creative hub in Paradise Street.

Terry and Jo, who is now head distiller, make their gins in the Baltic Triangle where their main still, Jasmine, is a mix of stainless steel and copper with a Carter Head for infusing the botanicals. There are small copper stills for doing blends for mixing and equipment for bottling and presentation, which is all done in-house.

In 2020, Turncoat opened a bar in the basement of Liverpool's historic Royal Albert Dock. Once a cognac store, the space with its brick arches has been transformed and there is a selection of draft beers on tap alongside the gins, wood-fired pizzas and bottle shop. It features eye-catching artwork by city-based mural artist Jazz Stan. In 2022, Terry opened a sister bar at 23 Hope Street on the edge of the city's Georgian Quarter.

WEETWOOD DISTILLERY
[Weetwood Gin]

Kelsall, Cheshire
www.weetwoodales.co.uk
First gin: October 2018

Weetwood is something special as it is one of those rare grain-to-glass distilleries. It makes its own spirit from barley mashed in its own brewhouse before creating its gins with it. Weetwood started life in 1992 as a brewery in a barn in the hamlet of the same name before moving to a larger purpose-built site nearby. Best known for its Cheshire Cat and Eastgate ales, it now brews more than 1.5 million pints of beer a year and employs a dozen staff.

In 2014, the founders, Adrian Slater and Roger Langford, sold the business to Phil McLaughlin and Laura Humby, a brother and sister with backgrounds in sales and finance. Phil had a passion for beer but neither sibling had experience of brewing or distilling before they were chosen to continue the founders' vision for quality and consistency.

They extended the buildings and, with a long-held ambition to produce a single-malt whisky, they set up the distillery in 2018. They purchased a copper still, custom-built to their precise design from Kothe in Germany. Like many whiskymakers, they launched a gin and vodka as they waited for the whisky to mature. Making their own Weetwood spirit means they do not buy in a neutral grain spirit as many ginmakers do.

The Weetwood London Dry gin has prominent juniper with vibrant citrus from its 16 botanicals which include bitter and sweet citrus peels. The botanical basket is positioned immediately before the condenser to pick up as much flavour as possible. The gin is left to mature for three weeks before being bottled on-site.

Raspberries are the hero ingredient in Weetwood's second gin. They and the juniper are gently macerated overnight in the Weetwood spirit before being slowly distilled with 15 other botanicals, some suspended in the still's basket. New in 2022 is a flavoured gin made with marmalade from Mrs Darlington's, a family business based in Crewe, with Elderflower and Sloe gins to follow. And there is rum and apple brandy, as well as ready-to-drink cans of pre-mixed spirits. Weetwood's first whisky is due to be bottled in late 2022.

WHITEHALL DISTILLERY
[Whitehall Distillery Signature, Riverside Gin]

Darwen, Lancashire
www.whitehalldistillery.co.uk
First gin: March 2021

Lancashire's first hotel-based distillery is a marriage made in heaven for Neil and Tracey Bullows, who run the Whitehall Hotel in Darwen. The idea of introducing ginmaking to the popular wedding venue came when the Covid lockdown wiped out their core business. The idea of building something which would diversify their income led Neil to contact Paul Sheerin at Defiance Distillery in Oldham, whom he had known since childhood. The distiller agreed to help and guided his old school friend through the process of making gin and building a distillery.

The pandemic gave Neil time to repurpose a redundant kitchen in the Victorian country house hotel into a distillery where he uses Cuff and

Link, his two 25-litre T500 stills to make the Whitehall Distillery Signature Gin. It has 17 botanicals, including tiger nuts, persimmon fruit and whinberries which are abundant in the surrounding countryside.

The labels celebrate the area's heritage, featuring the Darwen Tower which opened in 1898 to celebrate both Queen Victoria's Diamond Jubilee and a legal victory which secured the right of access to the moorland footpaths. The labels' background is inspired by the lace collars worn by Oliver Cromwell, who stayed in a cottage near the hotel the night before the Battle of Preston in 1648.

Neil takes the Signature gin to make fruit flavoured 30% ABV spirits, using orchard fruits in one and blood orange, kaffir limes and basil in another. Simply Pink is a 23% ABV

creation with raspberries, peach, English rose and honey. In his first year distilling, Neil won the opportunity to create a gin for Blackburn Rovers. Named after the stand beside the River Darwen, Riverside Gin teams up 14 botanicals for the football club's first gin. He is also working on a range of gins to celebrate the art of East Lancashire.

The Whitehall range is proving popular, particularly with the wedding guests who find personalised favours at their table or enjoy gin-themed pampering sessions. Also proving popular are the ginmaking sessions at the gin academy which has been created in a former swimming pool.

WILD FOX DISTILLERY
[Ivy's Signature, Twelve Bore, Blushing Vixen, It's a Rum Do]

Inglewhite, Lancashire
wildfoxdistillery.co.uk
First gin: April 2019

Farming is often a family business and Lower Barker – a thriving dairy farm – is now on to its fourth generation. Since 2018, alongside the milk from 450 Holstein cows another type of drink has been produced. It was then that Rob and Lizzie Billington created Wild Fox Distillery and started making gin.

The idea was kindled by the family tradition of a post-milking G&T and ignited with Lizzie's background in product development and the idea of creating a farm-to-bottle gin from the wealth of fruits and botanicals in the farm's orchard and hedgerows.

The couple researched the idea. Rob with his expertise in agricultural engineering concentrated on finding a still, while Lizzie honed the recipe on a table-top still, named Willow after their home.

A micro distillery was created to accommodate Ivy, a specially commissioned 50-litre copper column still and launch their first gin. Ivy's Signature is citrusy with a herbal zest from the golden raspberry leaves in the fresh botanical mix cut on the farm. There is also a special smoothness developed in Ivy's slow continuous distillation. Rob and

Lizzie called the distillery Wild Fox after their two "little red-headed feral farm kids".

Seasonal gins followed, making use of the rich harvest on their doorstep. Alongside Ivy's Signature, their year-round repertoire includes Twelve Bore, a 45% ABV orange zest and ginger gin and Blushing Vixen. The 40% ABV pink gin is distilled with farm-grown rhubarb and elderflowers from beside the brook, with its unique natural colour coming from the addition of powdered beetroot.

All the gins use grain spirit, but the process for each product is different. This is well illustrated with It's a Rum Do, a dark spiced gin which is double distilled before being vapour infused with dandelion heads and then aged in oak barrels for 10 months.

As farmers, being sustainable and caring for their surroundings is a way of life for Lizzie and Rob. They harvest botanicals from the farm, heat the distillery with biomass technology, use water from their own borehole and reuse it for the animals.

In April 2021, a larger distillery and shop opened to the public, allowing the Billingtons to share their farm-to-bottle experience with visitors. Guests can attend gin school or have afternoon tea and the larger space – with Kin, Ivy's twin still, installed – means scope for private label distilling and more seasonal gins.

ZYMURGORIUM
[Zymurgorium The Original Manchester Gin, The Cub]

Irlam, Greater Manchester
zymurgorium.com
First gin: January 2013

Zymurgorium is a name to catch the eye – it is an amalgamation of "zymurgy" – the study of scientific brewing – and "emporium" – a shop that sells various items and trinkets. It is a good fit for the brand which includes the Original Manchester Gins, liqueurs, craft beers, cider, mead and a bar, Project Halcyon in the former Granada TV studios in Manchester.

Central to all this is the distillery in Irlam where state-of-the-art production and bottling facilities mean enough capacity to produce nearly 70 million bottles a year across its range of more than 30 spirits and liqueurs.

The founder, Aaron Darke, started out as a shed-based mead-maker in 2012, before taking advantage of winning a £10,000 grant in a young entrepreneurs' competition and investing in distilling and brewing equipment, creating Manchester's first modern craft distillery. He now works with his father, David, and brother, Callum. His main still is a 2,000-litre packed column hybrid and there is a 400-litre wooden-clad copper still with three bubble plates at Project Halcyon.

The Original Manchester Gin is complex thanks to its 20 botanicals which include some unusual – and secret – ingredients and smooth from being made with Zymurgorium's Manchester vodka. In total there are nine full-strength craft gins, with one of the best sellers being Marmalade Gin which uses Seville marmalade from the Manchester firm Duerr's in the distillation, along with tangerine to get both bitter and sweeter notes.

You have to expect innovative flavours from Aaron, who studied microbiology and zoology at university, and another full-strength gin that pushes the boundaries is Syllabub Lime Gin which is described as "full frontal lemon, lime and pine with a note of warm oats". A collaboration with Beartown Breweries of Congleton in Cheshire, created The Cub – a "new" Old Tom style gin which pairs gently distilled Citra and Mosaic hops, with the juniper, lemon, lime and vanilla. In the pipeline is a range of gins aimed at a new and different market.

Zymurgorium's other spirits are as imaginative as they come, with its Parma Violet gin liqueur and Ruby Chocolate rum leading the way as world firsts. Manquila is a wild strawberry cream liqueur with agave spirit.

The full-strength craft gins are presented in tall, black glass bottles and the labels feature Manchester's worker bee which reflects the hard work that has gone into building the Zymurgorium brand.

THE KITH & KIN

Kith (one's friends or acquaintances) and Kin (one's relatives)

The Kith & Kin are the gins and makers who don't qualify for the Distilling Clan. They come from a variety of backgrounds across the North West of England.

The majority are gins created by people in the North West but made by someone else in an established distillery, which may be in the North West or elsewhere. The creators of these gins might be making them for their shops, hotels, visitor attractions or events. For others, they are commercial brands in their own right. Some of the gins use botanicals picked from their home area or they might be inspired by the creator's heritage or home village.

Among the Kith & Kin, there are also distillers who are in the process of setting up there own distillery but are not yet in production. Then there are "cuckoo distillers" who use distilling equipment belonging to other distillers.

Bathtub gin doesn't require a still to make it, so these makers are included here. They cold compound botanicals or fruit usually over a number of weeks or months to create gins bottled at a minimum of 37.5% ABV (alcohol by volume).

While we have tried to find every gin in the region, there are plenty of omissions. Not only are new gins launched with amazing regularity, but some successfully hide their light under the proverbial bushel.

AGNES ARBER

A pioneering botanical historian is the inspiration for this gin from one of the UK's largest independent drinks companies which has its UK headquarters in Oldham. Born in 1879 in London, Agnes Arber dedicated her life to discovering the intricacies and wonders of the natural world. With an academic focus on flowering plants, Agnes published many books and her work was well respected. In 1948, she was the first woman botanist to be elected as a Fellow of the Royal Society.

The Agnes Arber gins celebrate her work, using nine botanicals to balance the juniper with orange, lemon and liquorice notes. The Original gin is infused with fruit juice after distillation for the blushing Rhubarb Gin. Meanwhile Agnes Arber Pineapple Gin adds both mango and pineapple for a tropical take.

The gins, which are made at Langley Distillery in the West Midlands, come from the drinks wholesaler, LWC. Founded more than 40 years ago by Robin Gray and Ebrahim Mukadam, LWC has 14 depots across the country and under its Signature Brands name holds a portfolio of well-known products including Marlish spring water, Old J Rum, Monin fruit syrups and Bangla beer.

AGRIGENTO GIN

Liverpool
www.carlisi.co.uk
Launched: December 2021

In search of a fusion of Sicily and Liverpool for their bar on Dale Street, the Carlisi brothers have created Agrigento, a gin featuring lemons, oranges and a pinch of sea salt.

It is perfect for the bar which was opened by Alessio and Federico Carlisi in 2018 with the dream of bringing authentic Italian food and drink to the heart of Liverpool. Carlisi is the place to go for homemade cannoli or arancini and cheese, wine or meat imported directly from the best Italian suppliers.

Agrigento Gin is named after the brothers' home town, the hilltop city in the south-west of Sicily, known for the impressive ruins of the ancient city of Akragas, an extensive site with several Greek temples. The gin is made at

Murphy's Distillery in Liverpool using ingredients sourced from Sicily, with the lemons and oranges hand-prepared by a member of the Carlisi family.

AQUA SATIVA HAZY DRY GIN

Stockport, Cheshire
aquasativa.co.uk
Launched: November 2019

The cannabis or marijuana plant, Cannabis sativa, has been around for thousands of years and has found many uses over time. CBD (cannabidiol) is one of the chemical compounds found in it and is often associated with health and wellbeing. Unlike another of the plant's compounds, THC (tetrahydrocannabinol), CBD is not psychoactive.

It was the founder of Aqua Sativa, entrepreneur Paul Hesketh, who had the vision of adding CBD to the nation's favourite spirit to create a "disruptive alternative drink". Hazy Dry Gin takes its spiced notes from cinnamon, coriander and ginger, while the citrus balance comes from fresh orange, lemon, and grapefruit peel.

In Hazy Strawberry Gin, the fruit teams up with the original for a fruity summer edition. Both are infused with CBD from authorised and regulated suppliers in the UK, which is scientifically tested to be accurately dosed and free of THC. Hazy Gin – and vodka and rum – are made for Aqua Sativa by Alcohol Solutions in Manchester.

ATLAS BAR GIN

Manchester
atlasbarmanchester.com
Launched: June 2021

When you own the most famous gin bar in the city, it is only time before you launch your own gin. The fact that Mark and Elaine Wrigley had owned the Atlas Bar in Deansgate for almost a decade before they put their name on a gin is the only surprise.

They launched with the Atlas Bar Premium Small Batch London Dry Gin. Created in collaboration with Defiance Spirits in Oldham, its 19 botanicals include raspberries, lemon myrtle, spruce tips, lemon, orange, cinnamon quills, almonds, honey, lemongrass, allspice and cranberries. Manchester Strength captures the attitude of the city and, when they were developing this near-Navy strength recipe, they found that the city's latitude of 53.4 degrees north was also the perfect ABV to bottle it at.

Atlas Bar had been founded in 1996 and quickly became the stop before clubbing at the nearby Haçienda, the iconic venue of the 1980s and 1990s. When Mark and Elaine took it over in 2012 they spotted that gin was on the up and set about creating the popular gin bar we find today. As they recall, they launched with 28 gins "which was 21 more than anyone in Manchester city centre had at the time". Today the number is approaching 600 and it is home to the monthly gin supper club, as well as a specialist online bottle store, the Gin Bible.

BASHALL SPIRITS

Bashall Eaves, Lancashire
www.bashallspirits.co.uk
Launched: September 2019

Family recipe books are a rich part of our heritage. They can also provide inspiration for ginmakers. For Bashall Spirits co-founder Fiona McNeill, her relatives have left her a wealth of material to work with. Among her collection she has two recipe books – one from 1750 and the other from about 100 years later.

Wanting to capture the essence of her family home, Bashall Eaves, an agricultural estate in the Forest of Bowland, she turned to the beautifully handwritten books and, working with consultant distiller, Lewis Scothern of Distillutions in Arbroath, Scotland, had four gins created.

The Bashall Spirits London Dry is based on botanicals found in the countryside around Bashall Eaves. Cob nuts give the gin its smoothness, while cranberries grow in the village wildlife reserve and elderflowers fill the hedgerows in spring. Caraway is a common flavour in Lancashire dishes and grows profusely along roads and in the fields. Together 11 botanicals create a smooth juniper-forward gin with a soft sweetness.

The three flavoured gins link directly to the family recipes. Orange & Quince Gin is based on marmalet – the 18th-century term for marmalade, while Damson & Elderberry Gin is inspired by damson wine from the same era.

Every family had a recipe for parkin, the treacle and ginger cake that is traditional in Lancashire and Yorkshire, and Fiona's family is no different. The recipe she has used to inspire Bashall's Parkin Cake Gin is from a book written by her great-times-five grandmother Jennet.

BEDROCK GIN

Cumbria's first gin was launched in 2008 by Vince Wilkins, who was at the time a regional sales manager for a major alcohol supplier. Vince and design engineer Tim Moor – who went on to launch Langton's No1 in 2012 – had a vision of an exceptionally smooth, clean and contemporary London Dry gin. It was brought to life for their company, Spirit of the Lakes, by Natalie Wallis and her team at Langley Distillery in the Midlands.

The name Bedrock Gin was chosen to convey the elemental properties of the spirit and reflects that landscape of the Lake District where Vince grew up. The signature gin uses Cumbrian spring water and 13 botanicals, including oak bark, which are macerated overnight before distillation.

For years, Vince was committed to his signature London-style Bedrock Gin but eventually relented as the growth in flavoured gin took hold and he launched Gooseberry & Elderflower and Rhubarb Gin editions in 2019. He was clear that they would be classic fruit flavours, using his London Dry gin as the base liquid and bottled at 40% ABV. Bedrock Pink Gin launched in the summer of 2022.

Also in the Spirit of the Lakes portfolio is Bedrock Export Strength Gin bottled at 46% ABV and Standing Stones vodka which was launched in 2013, with a Berry Vodka being trialled more recently.

BEE-GINNING GIN CO

Ashton-under-Lyne, Lancashire
bee-ginning.co.uk
Launched: December 2020

Creating your own gin proved the perfect new direction for Dave and Ang Gandy when Covid knocked the wheels off their business. They had been running a popular mobile bar and hosting scaled-down gin festival events, even appearing on reality television, when the pandemic parked them up.

Instead of sitting it out, they discussed the idea of creating their own gins with Phil Smith of Ginsmith Manchester. The results are Bee-Ginning Premium, a traditional gin which is smooth and refreshing with bursts of blueberry and black sambuca berry, and the Navy strength Queen Bee.

Then, like the Manchester worker bee which features in their logo, Dave, who has a background in engineering and Ang, who is in car sales, got busy coming up with further Manchester-themed full-strength gins. The names might be eye-catching but the flavours don't overpower the juniper. There's Simply Red, Toffee Apple, Parma Violet, Twistin' my Melon, Top Banana, Cool Cucumber and Relight my Fire, where chilli peppers add heat to the Premium gin. Post-pandemic, the mobile gin business is back on the road and their own gins are in the driving seat.

BLACKPOOL ROCK GIN

Lytham St Annes, Lancashire
blackpoolrockgin.com
Launched: March 2019

A stick of rock is the very essence of a day at the seaside. And in Blackpool Rock Gin the fun and flavour of one of our most famous resorts have been captured in a bottle. The gin adds a dash of real Blackpool rock to a premium signature spirit.

The rock which comes from one of the town's oldest makers, Blackpool Rock & Novelties, gives the pink gin a balanced subtle sweetness and a peppermint finish. It is presented in a slim tall bottle, which is inspired by the other icon of the Lancashire coast – Blackpool Tower – and designed by Lytham-based creative, Jay Harrison.

Blackpool Rock Gin is made by gin consultant, Simon Smith, at a distillery in Lancashire. He brings a lifetime of experience in the spirits industry – including a senior management position at Langley Distillery – to create the range which includes Tutti Frutti, a gin featuring natural tropical fruit extracts.

To commemorate the 125th anniversary in 2019 of both the Blackpool Tower and the Grand Theatre, a limited edition showcased Simon's signature spirit, which is a traditional juniper-led spicy London Dry, made with 10 botanicals in small batches.

CAMINO GIN

Winsford, Cheshire
caminogin.com
Launched: November 2020

Tom Cartwright first walked the pilgrims' route to the Cathedral of Santiago de Compostela in 2016. He had recently dropped out of university and the 800km Camino Frances from the French Pyrenees to Santiago in the north-west of Spain was an education. He learned about life from fellow pilgrims and discovered the plants, fruits, mushrooms and herbs native to the Camino as it passes through different landscapes.

After a stint learning to make cocktails in Barcelona, Tom set up a mobile bar out of a 1970s VW campervan at the same time as working as a ghost tour guide in Bath. Back on home turf in Cheshire, he is now a sales executive for a brewery. But the pilgrimage had left its mark and he dreamed of creating a gin with botanicals from the Camino Frances.

Tom linked up with David Clayton and Ben Kaberry at Big Hill Distillery in nearby Mobberley to create Camino Gin. Made on their 130-litre copper still, 13 of its 17 botanicals can be found on the Camino Frances. The nettles, figs, wild cherry bark, lemon balm, lavender, bilberry and citrus fruits create a gin with a floral nose, together with a citrus and herbaceous flavour. Bottled in a glass flask, Tom believes it embodies the spirit of the Camino.

CHESHIRE BOTANICALS
[Nantwich Gin, Matron's Strength, Sweet Briar]

Nantwich, Cheshire
cheshirebotanicals.co.uk
Launched: November 2020

In the 17th century, the book to turn to if you needed to know anything about plants was written by John Gerard, a herbalist in the court of King James I. His Cheshire birthplace is now celebrating his expertise in botanicals with a gin. Developed by the Challinor family, Nantwich Gin is inspired by the botanicals Gerard would have grown in his herb garden. Juniper-forward, it combines lemon thyme, cardamom and pink peppercorns, with floral notes from lavender and rose.

Holly Challinor and her parents, Paul and Deb, developed the recipe on a six-litre iStill during the 2020 lockdowns. For Holly, a recent university graduate, it meant not just studying distilling techniques but also learning how to get a product to market. Nantwich Gin is now made for them by an unnamed distillery 22 miles away, although they hope to make it themselves in the future.

Paul, a horticultural consultant, brought his expertise in food production, including intensive hydroponics and vertical farming, to the table and they grow some of their botanicals using indoor farming techniques.

Deb is the inspiration behind Cheshire Botanicals' second gin, Matron's Strength, which was developed during the tough months of 2021. She is an NHS matron with 40 years' experience in nursing. The gin is bottled at 57% ABV to honour the bravery and tenacity of healthcare professionals.

Sweet Briar Gin, which marks the summer of 2022, gets its colour and sweetness from steeped blackberries. Its name is a nod to Nantwich's Sweet Briar Hall where Joseph Priestley, a philosopher and chemist who is credited with discovering oxygen, lived in the 1700s.

The labels for all the gins, which are designed by Jiri Borsky, a Czech-born artist based in Staffordshire, are inspired by Nantwich's Tudor architecture. The company's Cheshire cat logo was created by Paper Anchor Designs and it has been nicknamed Lewis, after the author Lewis Carroll, who was born in nearby Daresbury.

CUMBERLAND SAUCY GIN

Pooley Bridge, Cumbria
chestnuthouseonline.co.uk
Launched: September 2018

If you are looking for g-inspiration then Pooley Bridge is the place for you. At any one time there will be at least 450 bottles of gin on the shelves of Chestnut House, the off-licence grocers run by Andrew and Emma Kaye.

The pretty little village at the top of Ullswater is a destination in itself and now it is back on the map, thanks to a striking stainless steel bridge built after the devastating floods of December 2015, it is thriving.

Andrew and Emma, with their shop manager Darren Todd, have become such gin experts, that you can't help but linger as they share their encyclopedic knowledge beside their wall of gin.

It was inevitable that Andrew would want to create his own gin. Working with Andrew Emmerson at Solway Spirits in Dumfriesshire, he designed a gin based on Cumberland sauce, the savoury-sweet redcurrant sauce traditionally served with cold meat.

Using juniper, redcurrant, orange peel, black peppercorns, mustard seeds and coriander, Cumberland Saucy's simple recipe has created a contemporary gin which celebrates Cumberland traditions.

A recent makeover of the bottle by Cumbrian graphic designer and brand consultant Gary Lawson, highlights the curves of the fells that surround the shop's location.

DIDSBURY GIN

Greater Manchester
didsburygin.com
Launched: April 2017

This is the gin which put the Manchester suburb of Didsbury on the map when the founders, Liam Manton and Mark Smallwood, won the support of a TV dragon. On *Dragon's Den* in 2018, Hyde-born businesswoman, Jenny Campbell who went to school in Didsbury, backed their vision of natural fruit-infused, vegan-friendly craft gins.

Their journey had started when Liam moved to Didsbury and met Mark and they became friends over their shared love of gin. They felt they couldn't find exactly what they were looking for in a gin – namely a fresh, crisp taste. They set about exploring how to create that profile themselves. When they produced a small batch of gin to their taste in Liam's front room, the brand was born. The *Dragon's Den* investment came after the men had both found themselves jobless. Liam was redundant from a construction firm where he had started as an apprentice and Mark had lost his bar manager's job.

Their Original Didsbury Gin – now made by City of Manchester Distillery – is the heart of their range. Its 11 botanicals give well-defined juniper notes followed by fresh citrus from bitter orange, lime and grapefruit, making that clean, crisp and zesty gin they were seeking.

The Original is used in their range of full-strength gins made with real fruit: Raspberry & Elderflower, Blood Orange & Ginger, Strawberry & Sicilian Lemon, plus limited editions Peach & Rose, Plum & Rosehip and British Bramble. Slightly further from their original vision is the Manchester Tart Gin which, after a burst of raspberry, gives way to vanilla and a hint of coconut, underpinned by juniper.

The brand – part of Alderman's Drinks – has gone from strength to strength with listings in major retailers and bars, cocktail cans launched, Arlu rum added to the range and export markets explored.

HUNTERS CHESHIRE GIN

Crowley, Cheshire
www.huntersgin.com
Launched: November 2012

Apples from an ancient Cheshire orchard are at the core of Hunters gin. The apple of choice is Arthur Barnes, a cross between Gascoyne's scarlet and Cox's orange pippin created by NF Barnes in 1902, the Duke of Westminster's gardener. The versatile apple was named after his son who died in the First World War and is buried in Eccleston churchyard near Chester.

They were growing in the gardens at Norton Priory, the ecclesiastical site in Runcorn founded in 1134. The home of the Brooke family from 1545 to 1921, it has a 2.5-acre Georgian walled garden where apples, pears and the national collection of quince grow.

The gin was the idea of Ian Cass and Jon Jones, friends who worked in the spirits industry. They wanted to create a gin that "you could enjoy from early in the day, in a good cocktail at night and suited the Cheshire lifestyle". Based on a 300-year-old recipe, they made the Arthur Barnes apple their hero ingredient. And now they are harvested from an orchard planted at Jon's farm.

Made at the Langley Distillery in the Midlands, Hunters Gin's botanicals include lemon and sweet orange peels, ground nutmeg from the West Indies, French angelica and Madagascan cinnamon bark. The 43.3% ABV gin has subtle citrus overtones with a spicy, fruity edge and its translucent bottles are inspired by old-fashioned ginger ale.

In 2016, Ian made way for a new managing director, Bill Allen, who has a background in the health and beauty industry. Aside from an elegant brand makeover, Hunters Cheshire Gin remains unchanged, although it is now also available as a ready-to-drink G&T in a can.

KINGDOM'S GIN

Chester, Cheshire
kingdomrecommends.co.uk
Launched: April 2020

Kingdom Thenga has come a long way from picking lychees for his grandmother in South Africa. Along the way he found himself homeless in London, given a lifeline by a stranger and working in pubs in Manchester before running his own bars. Guiding him in his business is the spirit of "ubuntu", a South African term meaning "humanity to others" which also translates into "I am what I am because of who we all are" and from that comes his philosophy to give back to his community and provide a neighbourliness that welcomes all. It is how he runs his bars around Chester.

An introduction to distiller Chris Toller of Henstone in Shropshire allowed Kingdom to realise a dream of having his own range of gins. Together they developed the recipe for Kingdom's London Dry Gin. Smooth enough to sip, it has orange and lemon peels, alongside traditional botanicals and a tiny amount of hops which give a fragrant, warm overtone.

Also in the Kingdom Recommends range are a Navy strength Ginger Spiced, Orange & Nutmeg and Organic Morello Cherry gins, as well as a vodka and a spiced rum. And in Luscious Lychee Gin, Kingdom evokes those days picking the fruit for his grandmother to take to market. Presented with striking animal designs on the labels, the bottles also raise funds for animal charities.

LANGTONS NO1 GIN

The Lake District
www.langtonsgin.co.uk
Launched: December 2012

Langtons of Skiddaw No 1 was created as a Lake District gin, making use of Cumbria's rich resources. There is water filtered through the slate of Skiddaw, the 3,054ft mountain in its name, and bark from ancient Lakeland oak trees among its 11 botanicals.

This creates a smooth sippable gin with a clear citrus note which is shown off in bespoke square bottles from Allied Glass in Leeds. Inspired by greenish-blue Cumbrian slate, the bottles capture the contours of the fells in their tactile sides.

It was Tim Moor, a designer, and Nick Dymoke-Marr, a drinks industry professional, who had the idea of creating a Lake District gin which they honed with the help of wine writer Joe Wadsack and master distiller Joanne Moore at G&J Distillers in Warrington.

Today, the gin is owned by a group of friends who loved it so much that they bought the brand in 2019. Still made by G&J, Sarah McDonald and her friends are looking at their options after the interruption of the pandemic.

MOTHER GIN

Liverpool
m0ther.co.uk
Launched: March 2019

Alishia Thomas has created a gin devoted to the most important women in our lives. Infused with cherry blossom, Sicilian lemon and hints of lavender, this is designed to celebrate motherhood. Cherry blossoms are associated with beauty and the birth of new life but they are also a reminder to enjoy every single moment of it because, as every mother knows – or will find out – babies aren't little for long.

In fact, Alishia has more expertise on the subject than most, having founded a freelance agency, M0ther, after she spotted a gap in the employment market for working mothers in the creative industries. She has since gathered a portfolio of bespoke gifts for mothers.

When she wanted to create a gin that represented the agency's brand and ethos she turned to Turncoat in Liverpool with a very specific flavour in mind. Together they finessed the recipe and created M0ther Gin. Described as bold, playful and feminine, it works just as well in cocktails as it does as a sipping gin. A Winter edition adds festive notes from winterberries, blackberries and sloes. And look out for ready-to-drink options.

PENNINE GIN

Mellor, Cheshire
www.penninegin.co.uk
First gin: September 2019

At the southern end of the Pennines, Kinder Scout, is as iconic a mountain as they come. Scene of the Mass Trespass of 1932 which ultimately opened up the hills for subsequent generations, Kinder Scout is only 20 miles from Manchester. Within sight of it, Alex Brown and Oli Meadows are setting up a micro distillery where they will produce their Pennine gins.

Working around their day jobs in property development, the school friends are making gin on small stainless steel and copper pot stills, having started out in a garage. Since relinquishing premises during Covid, they have been looking for somewhere permanent for their Brown & Meadows Distillery, hoping that it will also be able to hold gin tastings or maybe a gin bar. A bespoke copper 250-litre still made by an engineering firm in Compstall is due by the autumn of 2022.

Their journey started after Oliver's hobby of making sloe gin with off-the-shelf gin had expanded to making a London Dry gin using botanicals. He and Alex tried his recipes on friends and family which went down very well, so they went to the next level and registered the name and created the brand Pennine Gin. Everything is handcrafted from the preparing of ingredients to the bottling and the application of labels and seals.

Their Original gin has 20 botanicals, including juniper, coriander, cassia bark, liquorice root, fennel, orange, lemon and lime peels, almonds and lavender, which are vapour infused and combined with pure mineral water from the Buxton spring in the Pennines. It is well balanced with lemon, orange and aniseed on the nose and juniper, spice and citrus on the palate.

To expand the range, they vapour infuse additional flavours in a basket with the original gin. There is Citrus with tangy oranges, lemons, limes and grapefruit; Forest Fruits with blueberries, blackberries and raspberries and Pennine Pink uses raspberries, strawberries and fragrant rose petals. They also add a fiery kick to the Original by steeping spicy Scotch bonnet chillies in it to create their Chilli Pennine Gin.

RASCAL PREMIUM GIN

Liverpool
www.rascalgin.co.uk
Launched: March 2019

Musician Dan Walsh discovered craft gin almost by accident. He was a college music teacher and playing guitar for a band, Random Hand, when he ended up working on a bar for Gin Festival in 2014.

Dan had worked many more events and honed his gin knowledge when changes at the college gave him the opportunity, in 2017, to commit to Gin Festival and join its Tinker Gin project.

When Gin Festival and Tinker Gin folded, Dan started to explore the idea of doing a gin himself – aiming for high quality but also wanting it to be as authentic, honest, fun and unpretentious as possible.

The name Rascal seemed to hit the right note and soon Dan was composing his own recipes and branding, working with Gin Festival contacts Adam Greasley of Oakfold Design and Tom Marshall of Hobo Tom Photography. Launched in March 2019, Rascal's original edition has classic citrus flavours from orange and lemon peels, lifted by passionfruit and a touch of raspberry.

When lockdown came, Dan had been working on a second expression, Blood + Passion. Again it has a citrus-driven base, but with passionfruit and layers of orange and blood orange. A Covid challenge meant a change in distillery was necessary and he turned to Locksley Distilling Co in Sheffield. In true "cuckoo" style, Dan felt totally in tune with John Cherry and his team as he transferred his recipes and distilled his first batches there.

He has since developed the recipe for a third Rascal gin – Pepper Berry, which sings with zesty citrus, bold raspberry and aromatic pink peppercorn notes. Although Dan really enjoys distilling, with a band to play in, he is happy to let Locksley look after the production while he composes new recipes.

TIRRIL GINS

Long Marton, Cumbria
tirrilbrewery.uk
Launched: December 2018

The revelation that gin does not need to taste synthetic, was a game changer for Chris Tomlinson, founder of Tirril Brewery. The chef-turned-brewer was talking to Andrew Emmerson of Solway Spirits in Dumfriesshire, when he found out that if he supplied a "real" flavour Andrew could turn it into a gin.

Together they set about devising 40% ABV gins using ingredients on Chris's doorstep. He makes the syrups from them in his kitchen. There are gins made from the rosehips, sloes and blackberries of the Cumbrian hedgerows. Elderflower Gin is sweetened with honey from a farm deep in the Borrowdale valley. Tirril's Farmhouse gins feature rhubarb, raspberries and lovage from the kitchen garden where ducks roam and they use hops from the brewery to fertilise the soil.

Some of the botanicals that Chris forages are rare. He finds wild juniper berries in the Lake District, while the golden raspberries he collects make so few bottles each year that it is only sold at the National Trust's Sticklebarn tavern in the Langdale valley. Another rare plant in the Lake District is bog myrtle which is used in schnapps in mainland Europe, and Chris hopes to make a wild myrtle gin soon. For Bonfire Toffee Gin, Chris took his inspiration from his Grandma Howarth's recipe so that when mixed with ginger ale you could be tasting traditional parkin.

Happy with the natural flavours, Chris launched the gins under his brewery's flag. With its commitment to authenticity and quality ingredients, Tirril is one of Cumbria's oldest independent breweries. Chris bought a pub in the village of Tirril near Ullswater in 1996 and launched the brewery there in 1999. It has since moved twice but still carries the name.

WOLFTOWN

Ulverston, Cumbria
www.wolftown.uk
Launched: November 2019

Capturing the spirt of home was at the heart of John McKeown's quest to create a gin. When the film cameraman thought about his childhood on the Furness peninsula to the west of Morecambe Bay it was Sass – the soda pop they drank – that lingered in his mind.

Made by Marsh & Son of Barrow-in-Furness until the late 1990s, sarsaparilla is a black-coloured soft drink made from the sarsaparilla plant which would have arrived at the local ports from the Americas. It is also a legacy of the temperance movement which was strong in the area.

So sarsaparilla had to be in John's contemporary gin along with other botanicals such as ginger, cinnamon and black pepper that would have arrived at the ports, as well as orange and lemon peel, ground almonds and goji berries. Appropriately the goji berries are also known as wolfberries.

He developed the recipe for Wolftown Signature Gin with Bottomley Distillers in Lincolnshire, and returned to them for his second – Citrus Gin – which was born out of a Lockdown yearning for the Mediterranean for John and his travel agent wife, Helen. The classic style pushes the citrus and uses Cumbrian milled organic oats, which replace the almonds of his signature gin but retain its creamy mouthfeel.

When he was looking for a name for his gin, he turned to his home town. Ulverston is derived from the Norse world "ulfarr", which means wolf warrior and "tun" a farm or homestead. And so Wolftown was born, with the help of Cumbria design company, Eclectic Creative. The striking wolf's head logo adorns the wall of the Wolfden – a shop and mircopub which John opened in Ulverston in 2020.

WORSLEY GIN

Worsley, Salford
www.worsleygin.co.uk
Launched: September 2017

Marrying dreams with technology can have impressive results. For the Duke of Bridgewater in 1761 it was using modern engineering to make his vision of a canal to link his coal mines in Worsley with the growing industrial centre of Manchester. Today the Royal Horticultural Society has been undertaking a massive project to create the RHS Garden Bridgewater at Worsley New Hall.

Inspired by the rich history of his home town, Andrew "Ned" Niedzwiecki has brought together state-of-the-art scientific processes, elegant design and high quality ingredients to bring his dream of a gin for Worsley to life.

Not content with a "taste profile", Ned's quest was for a "flavour journey". For that he turned to a master distiller, Dr John Walter of the English Spirit Company in Cambridgeshire. After an 18-month adventure, sampling more than 180 recipe variations, they were ready to launch Worsley Gin.

Its botanicals have been selected on three main principles – taste, scent and molecular structure. Understanding the structures allowed them to pair and combine botanicals to create the flavour journey for Ned, who has a science degree and a background in pharmaceuticals. The botanicals of the London Dry-style gin include pink grapefruit, mandarin leaf and coriander and from Worsley wild buttercups, dandelions and rose petals from Ned's father's garden.

The gin, which is now made by Marzio Di Rocco of the British Honey Company (BHC) in Buckinghamshire, is presented in rhomboid bottles with labels designed by Oveja & Remi Studio, a small agency in Argentina which works with drinks companies across the world. Having gained organic accreditation for Worsley Gin, Ned is working with BHC on applying for vegan accreditation as well.

Ned's next project has been developing a gin for RHS Garden Bridgewater which will be flavoured with botanicals grown there. Longer term, Ned's plan has been to learn from the best so that he can open a distillery and spirit experience in the heart of Worsley.

AUTHOR'S THANKS

I don't want to say that gin has taken over my life but it has grown from a bright idea for a writing project into serious research. Across the gin community I have had enormous support – the distillers, makers, owners, ambassadors and experts of every sort have been incredibly generous with their time. I won't single anyone out as that would be unfair, but I hope this book will repay their investment in me.

At Great Northern Books, David Burrill has come up with the striking cover for this book. I adore the way he has been inspired by the North West and has moved the design on from his clever take on Charles Rennie Mackintosh which graced The GIN CLAN's cover.

Thanks to my friends who continue to humour my fascination for botanicals and bottle design, attend gin events and happily help with a bit of tasting. The fact I'm now on my third book is testament to that support!

Fiona Laing
Edinburgh, July 2022

INDEX
Gins, makers and distilleries in the Clan and Kith & Kin listings

Yorkshire's Gins
by Fiona Laing

From the wild open spaces of the north to the industrial cities of the south, Yorkshire's distillers are creating some of the finest gins in the country. Discover how Yorkshire delicacies like rhubarb, liquorice and Henderson's Relish inspire the makers. See how brewers, farmers and artists have brought their talents to Yorkshire's gin community.

The Gin Clan
by Fiona Laing

In Scotland's gin scene a clan of distillers is creating passionately conceived and beautifully crafted gins, using the finest locally sourced ingredients. We tell the stories of the spirits, where Scotland's gin industry has come from and where it's going.

www.gnbooks.co.uk